E.C.L.A.T.
EUROPEAN CENTRE FOR LEARNING
AND TRAINING
7, avenue Albert Durand
31700 BLAGNAC
Tél. 05 61 15 63 63

EiD I.01.M

ENGLISH FOR INTERNATIONAL BANKING AND FINANCE

ENGLISH
FOR INTERNATIONAL
BANKING AND FINANCE

Jim Corbett

CAMBRIDGE
UNIVERSITY PRESS

PUBLISHED BY THE PRESS SYNDICATE OF THE UNIVERSITY OF CAMBRIDGE
The Pitt Building, Trumpington Street, Cambridge, United Kingdom

CAMBRIDGE UNIVERSITY PRESS
The Edinburgh Building, Cambridge CB2 2RU, UK   http://www.cup.cam.ac.uk
40 West 20th Street, New York, NY 10011–4211, USA   http://www.cup.org
10 Stamford Road, Oakleigh, Melbourne 3166, Australia

First published 1990
Ninth printing 1999

Printed in the United Kingdom at the University Press, Cambridge

ISBN 0 521 31999 4 Student's Book
ISBN 0 521 32000 3 Guide for Teachers
ISBN 0 521 26677 7 Cassette

For MTS

To the user

Who the book is for

This book is for people who need English for their day-to-day work in international banking, as well as for students of international banking and professional people whose work brings them into contact with international banking and finance.

How you can use this book

The book can be used in class, in one-to-one teaching and for self-study. If you are using the book on your own, you will need a copy of the *Guide for Teachers*. This contains background information on the banking and finance topics, an answer key and the tapescripts for the listening material on the cassette. Please note that if you are working on your own then you will not be able to do some of the communication activities, that is unless you can find a friend to do them with!

How the book is organized

There are nine thematically linked units. Unit 3, for example, has Foreign Exchange as its topic. These units are self-contained so they can be used on their own or grouped together to form modules according to individual needs.

The units are each divided into four sections. The first three sections in a unit are based on listening materials. The fourth section in a unit mainly contains reading texts. A unit provides between three and five hours work. They follow a consistent format so the book is easy to use. At the back of the book there is a list of abbreviations used in banking and finance.

How the cassette fits in

The listening material provides the main input for the first three sections of a unit. The great majority of the recordings are based on transcriptions of authentic recordings made on location in financial institutions.

Contents

Thanks

In preparing this book, I have received generous help and advice from a large number of people and organizations: my sincere thanks to all of them.

Special thanks are due to: Steffan Alvollin, Wilhelm Bergman, Ingemar Bergqvist, Michael Burmester, Janice Cowell, Bill Davis, Patrick Hanks, John Heywood, Alan Jones, Terry Laidlaw, Mickey Lowe, Terry Pope, Jan Sundgren and Paul Tucker, all of whom helped with source materials; also to Hambros Bank, National Westminster Bank, Nordic Bank, PK Christiania Bank (UK), Rank Xerox and KEY English Language Services AB.

My thanks are also due to the following people and organizations for piloting and commenting on my draft manuscript:

Sue Fortescue; Vivienne Ward; Doreen Lee at the Harven School of English in Woking, Surrey; Bill Horncastle at the Cambridge Centre for Languages; Eric Freedman at IFG Langues in Paris;
Vicky Mabbs and Jane Lawton at the Regent School in Rome;
Joe Wiersma at International House Executive Courses in London; Don Byron at Esade Idiomas in Barcelona; Saul Ray at Excellence Corporation in Tokyo; H Zak at Ecole Cadres in Courbevoie; Elizabeth Sim and Michael Sneyd at Eurocentre, Cambridge; G Marcy Bergqvist at KEY English Language Services in Stockholm; Jane Ferentzi-Sheppard at the VHS Language Centre in Nuremburg; Herbert Chang at Target in Sao Paulo;
Jan Janssen at Interlingua Talenpraktikum in Holland;
Anne Larsen at STE in Eindhoven; Vivienne Ward at Ebury Executive School; Hong Kong Polytechnic; Let's in Sao Paulo

Last but by no means least, my thanks are due to the publishing team at Cambridge University Press: Peter Donovan, Desmond O'Sullivan, Lindsay White and Will Capel.

Unit 1 Bank organization

This unit is about bank organizational structures and how to describe them. We will hear three bankers describing the structure of organizations they work for: banks of different types and sizes in different countries.

Section A   **A1**

Look through the following short report concerning the reorganization of a bank.

> The Allied Bank is reorganizing its operations into three business sectors: corporate banking and international banking operations will be headed by Bernard Rogers, who is currently Director of International Banking Operations and Deputy General Manager; the finance operations sector, including foreign exchange operations, short-term money market operations and accounting, will be headed by Lucy John, while David Lacey has been named Deputy General Manager with responsibility for the branch network and retail banking sector.

1   In the boxes below each name, fill in the division for which each person will be responsible. Beneath the boxes add any details which are given about the responsibilities of the divisions.

Bernard Rogers   Lucy John   David Lacey

2 Now look at the words in the left-hand column, which are taken from the text. Match them with words from the right-hand columns.

1 operations	A reports	G led
2 sectors	B at present	H offices
3 headed	C activities	I areas
4 currently	D sales	
5 including	E covering	
6 named	F appointed	

A2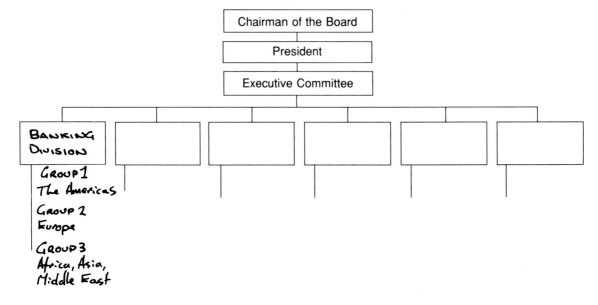

You are going to hear Ed Walker, an Assistant Vice-President of a large American bank, talking about the structure of his bank to Françoise Caie, a French banker. Before you listen to the conversation, look at these questions which you will answer after you have listened for the first time.

1 Is Ed:
   a) explaining the bank's organizational structure?
   b) discussing the bank's organizational structure?
2 Does Ed:
   a) give a basic outline of the bank's organizational structure?
   b) give a detailed analysis of the bank's organizational structure?

Now listen to Ed's conversation with Françoise.

A3

Listen again to what Ed says about the structure of his bank. As you do so, complete the following organization chart. Firstly, write in the boxes the names of the divisions. Then under the boxes add details of the responsibilities of each of the divisions.

Chairman of the Board

President

Executive Committee

BANKING DIVISION

GROUP 1
The Americas

GROUP 2
Europe

GROUP 3
Africa, Asia,
Middle East

A4

Look at the words in the box, all of which are from this section. Check any words that you do not know with a partner. Then, working together, match the words with the correct definition from the list below.

credit policy	bullion	consumers
annual report	line divisions	strategic planning
premises	personnel	commercial paper
domestic	reorganized	municipal bonds
comptroller's department		
investment portfolio management		

1 A report presented each year, giving details of the company's activities and financial performance during the previous financial year.
2 Formed or structured in a new way.
3 Sections of a company which deal with different products or services from each other.
4 People who buy goods or services.
5 In your own country, not abroad.
6 Management of a client's collected investments.
7 Short-term documents usually sold by big US corporations, promising to pay a specified sum of money on a particular date. They may be sold again by the buyer.
8 Documents issued by a local government authority, promising to repay loans at a certain time.
9 Bars of gold or silver.
10 Employees, staff.
11 Buildings and surrounding land.
12 A department which controls the internal finances of a company.
13 Deciding the main aims of an organization.
14 Plans for the lending of money.

Section B   **B1**

You are going to hear Clive Regis, the Director of a London merchant bank, being interviewed about his bank's organization. As you listen, look at these headings. Which ones does he talk about and in which order?

- Structure of the parent company
- Brief history of the bank
- Range of services provided
- Recent changes

B2

Listen again to what Clive says about the organization of the bank. As you do so, write in the boxes below the names of the six divisions to which he refers and list their main areas of responsibility.

Administration Division					

B3

Look at the terms in the left-hand column. Match each one with its correct definition in the right-hand column.

1 merchant bank

2 clearing bank

3 wholly-owned subsidiary

4 accounting and audit

5 syndicated loan

6 overdraft

7 documentary credit

8 correspondent banking

9 currency option

A The selling-off of interests.

B A very large loan for one borrower, arranged by several banks.

C Money overdrawn on bank accounts to agreed limits.

D Documents promising to pay sums of money at specified times.

E Money placed in countries with very low taxes.

F The joining of two or more companies into one.

G A bank which is a member of a central organization through which cheques are presented for payment.

H Activities where one bank acts as an agent for another bank.

I A contract where the buyer has the right to demand purchase or sale of a specified currency, but no obligation to do so.

10	bonds	J	A bank mainly concerned with the financing of international trade.
11	floating rate note	K	An organization which collects and pools money from many small investors and invests it in securities for them.
12	Eurodollar CD	L	A company entirely owned by another company.
13	financial futures	M	A limited company formed to invest in securities.
14	merger	N	A method of financing international trade where the bank accepts a bill of exchange from the exporter for the invoice amount, in return for receipt of the invoice and certain shipping documents.
15	takeover	O	The buying of a majority of the shares of companies.
16	divestment	P	Contracts to buy or sell currencies, bonds and bills, etc. at a stated price at some future time.
17	USM flotation	Q	Note on which interest rates are fixed periodically, and which can be traded on the market.
18	investment trust	R	Document given for a deposit repayable on a fixed date, the currency being dollars which are deposited outside the USA.
19	unit trust	S	The keeping of financial records and their periodic examination.
20	offshore funds	T	The starting of a new limited company, where the shares are not included in the official list on the Stock Exchange.

B4

Imagine that you are organizing a dinner party for 12 bank officials, including yourself. The other 11 people each work in different areas of banking, which are as follows:

Financial control
Investment management
Documentary credits
Planning
Overdrafts

Syndicated loans
Correspondent banking
Foreign exchange
Corporate finance
Accounting and audit
Project finance

Draw up a seating plan for the guests and yourself, placing everyone at the table below. When you have finished, compare your plan with that of a partner. Discuss any similarities and differences, and explain the reasons behind your plan.

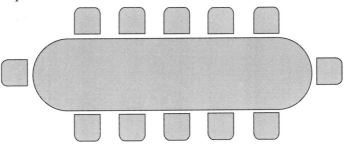

Section C   **C1**

So far we have heard about and looked at the structure of a large American bank and a British merchant bank. Now we are going to look at the work of a savings bank. Look at the following list of banking services. Put a tick (✔) next to those that are traditionally associated with savings banks.

Currency options	
Personal loans	
Safe-deposit services	
Takeovers	
Deposit accounts	
Bullion	
Payment of standing orders	
Cheque paying services	
Leasing packages	

C2

Now listen to Kai Larsen describing the organization of the Scandinavian savings bank he works for and fill in the organization chart below. Listen twice if necessary.

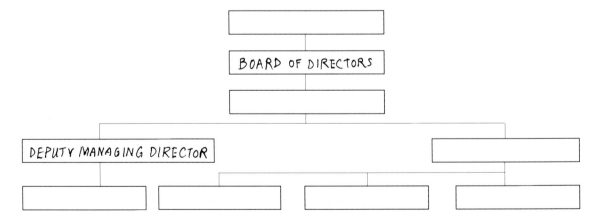

C3 🖭

Look at the following extracts from Kai's description of the savings bank. Work with a partner and note down what you think the speaker says instead of the words in *italics*. Then listen to the section again and compare your answers with the words Kai actually uses.

1 ... to understand just what we are and that is a .... (*bank set up to accept deposits from members of the public*)
2 ... . in 1878 ... (*set up, established*)
3 In 1980 we .... with the two largest regional savings banks ... (*joined together*)
4 ... and effectively this now gives us a .... to serve the private customer ... (*system of local offices over the whole country*)
5 There's a Board of Directors, which is elected by the Board of .... (*people responsible for administering money or property for the benefit of others*)
6 ... to gain access to the .... (*markets in which there are good profits*)
7 ... markets dominated by the .... (*banks which offer a wide range of services to the public, to companies and to other organizations*)
8 ... . 1970 ... (*before*)
9 ... couldn't accept deposits .... the equivalent of ... (*more than*)
10 ... granted an international .... of 45 million dollars ... (*loan of money at a fixed rate of interest, involving a certificate of the debt*)
11 ... and which had a .... 50 per cent of which ... (*an entire collection of loans*)
12 ... and expanding worldwide .... (*arrangements with banks who act for each other*)
13 ... major investments in terms of .... (*people who work here*)
14 ... necessary for us to be able to .... (*increase the range or extent of our operations*)

C4

You are going to make a short presentation of your bank or company. Look through the list of points below and decide in which order you will use them in your presentation. Then compare your order with that of a partner and discuss any differences.

- Range of services
- Financial performance
- Structure
- Specialized products
- Geographical representation

Now make a short presentation of the structure of your bank or company. Use any visual aids, such as diagrams, that will help you.

Section D   **D1**

Quickly read the text below, which is taken from an annual report of one of the world's largest banks. Then choose the best heading from this list.

The year in brief
Financial review
Global banking resources
Notes to the accounts
Foreign locations

To service the needs of different client groups effectively, the Bank is organized into three broad groups: the Domestic Banking Group, the Corporate Banking Group and the International Banking Group.

The basis of the Bank's strength continues to be its domestic banking operations. The Domestic Banking Group's network of 295 branches provides a full range of banking services nationwide and is the largest network in the country.

The Corporate Banking Group is responsible for servicing the complex needs of over 200 of the nation's largest corporations. Of the Bank's total domestic deposits and domestic loans outstanding, the Corporate Banking Group accounts for 25 per cent and 40 per cent respectively.

The Bank continues to develop and expand its international operations, and in fiscal 1991 foreign earnings surpassed those of the country's other leading banks for the fourth consecutive year. Since January 1 1990, the Bank has opened six new representative offices and has upgraded the Rome representative office into a full service branch. Our strong international presence is currently maintained through 12 branches, 18 representative offices, two agencies and 10 subsidiaries and affiliates.

The International Banking Group includes regional departments which assume responsibility as follows: the Americas; Africa, Middle East and Europe; Asia and Oceania. The Group includes both the Correspondent Banking Department, which is responsible for the Bank's correspondent banking network of some 1,500 institutions, and the Merchant Banking Department.

Also within this Group, the International Treasury Department specializes in foreign exchange and funding operations, while the International Planning Department is responsible for strategic planning. The International Business Supervision Department is responsible for the assessment of country risk and corporate credits, as well as for systems development and for ensuring compliance with regulations regarding international business.

The Bank continues to respond well to market dynamics both at home and abroad. Part of the Bank's strength lies in the wide spread of its representation and in its ability to develop sophisticated new services to meet the changing patterns in banking opportunities. The Bank's aim is to ensure the continued prosperity of the group by means of its dedication to service and by expanding the scope of its activities, both geographically and functionally. We believe that we have the right organization to do this in the period ahead.

D2

Using the information in the text you have just read, complete this organization chart.

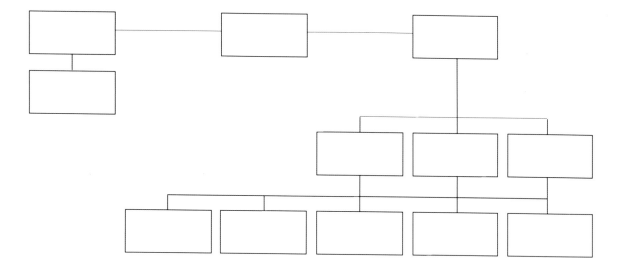

D3

Based on the information in the text, say whether the following statements are true or false.

1 The Corporate Banking Group services the needs of 1,500 of the nation's largest institutions.
2 The Corporate Banking Group plays an important part in terms of the bank's domestic deposits and domestic lending.
3 1991 was the fourth year in a row in which the bank earned more money abroad than any other bank in the country.
4 The bank has 30 branches and representative offices abroad.
5 The bank plans to increase its international operations.

D4

Read through the following information.

A commercial bank, a merchant bank, a savings bank and a clearing bank all have head offices on the same street in London.

The commercial bank and the clearing bank both have six business sectors.

The commercial bank, the savings bank and the clearing bank are all independent banks.

The bank with four line divisions was founded in 1920.

The bank which is a wholly-owned subsidiary is split into five line divisions.

The commercial bank was founded in 1928 and has a larger number of correspondent relationships than the other three banks.

The bank with the smallest number of personnel was established in 1896 and is no longer independent.

Given these facts, work out the following:

1 Which bank has four line divisions?
2 Which bank was formed by a merger in 1946?

D5

To end this unit, interview a partner about the organization of the bank he or she works for. Then write a description of the organization of this bank and give it to your partner to look through and comment on. If you all work for the same bank, then describe a bank you have worked for in the past or know well. You may need to do a little research!

Unit 2 Bank performance

In this unit we hear three different bankers presenting facts and figures concerning the recent financial performance of their banks.

Section A **A1**

First read the following short newspaper reports. Then from this list choose an appropriate headline for each report.

Profits forecast   **Mixed profits**

Fall in profits   **Growing debts**

Loss reported   **Profits growth**

1

Harborne Investment Bank has reported a loss equivalent to USD 295,000 for the first six months of 1991, a figure in line with the lower first-half earnings reported by the country's other leading banks. The bank posted a USD 2.86 million profit for fiscal 1990.

2

Hogg and Lacey's Bank has announced an income of USD 58 million for the first half of the year, an increase of 45 per cent over the corresponding period last year. The bank has increased its interim dividend from USD 1.50 to USD 1.80 a share.

3

Northland's FA Bank group increased operating results by 20 per cent to USD 108 million in the first six months of this year. Westsund Bank, in contrast, reported a drop to USD 80.5 million, while Quintorp Bank reported steady earnings of USD 195 million, but a 15 per cent fall in the parent bank figure to USD 178 million.

4

ZB Bank expects net profits in the region of CHF 33 million for the current financial year, according to Dr Fritz Ullmann, a rise of some 12 per cent. At the end of June the bank's balance sheet total was CHF 4.42 billion, compared with CHF 4.13 billion at the beginning of the year.

A2 📼

What main information about financial performance would you expect a representative of a bank to present to a company in order to try to sell the bank's services? Make a brief list. Then listen to Ed Walker give an informal presentation of his bank to a prospective client. Tick (✓) any points of yours which he makes.

A3 📼

Listen again to Ed talking about his bank's performance for the previous financial year. As you do so, fill in the spaces in the extract from the annual report below.

Highlights

$ In millions, except per share data

For the Year	1990	1989
Net Income	....	....
Net Interest Income	....	1,600
Per Share		
Net Income	....	4.80
At Year-End		
Assets	....	59,000
Deposits	....	34,700
Investment Securities	....	1,900
Employees	....	13,650
Number of Offices	....	1,150

A4 📼

Look at the following list. Work with a partner and note down what you think Ed says instead of the words in *italics*. Then listen to his presentation again and compare your answers with the words that Ed actually uses.

1 I have here a copy of our last *report presented each year, giving details of the company's activities and financial performance during the previous financial year.*
2 But I can give you right now a very *short general description* ...
3 ... based on *money received from the sale of the parts into which the capital of a company is divided* ...
4 ... and sixth largest based on *the sums of money left with the bank.*

5 ... financial services to a *large number of different types of customer* ...
6 ... which includes *company customers* ...
7 ... and *banks in other countries with whom we have an agency relationship.*
8 In 1990 we achieved *our highest ever profits after transfers to reserves* ...
9 ... our *tenth year in a row* of profit growth ...
10 *The annual income of the group of companies after the payment of costs* was 500 ...
11 ... at the end of 1990 *the value of all the things we own* ...
12 ... in *the financial year 1990* ...
13 ... billion dollars worth of *placements of money, for example in shares, so as to produce profit.*

A5

Say the following numbers. There may be alternative ways of saying some of them.

1 1,200
2 560,000,000
3 5,000,000,000
4 37,600,000
5 1,500,672
6 1,500,000

Section B B1

Look at the following expressions. Put a tick (✔) by the ones you might expect to hear in a presentation relating to financial performance and a cross (✗) by those you would not expect to hear. Then compare your answers with those of a partner and discuss any differences.

1 This diagram gives a very brief summary of some of the key figures.
2 Highlights from the audited financial statements as at 31 December 1990.
3 If we begin with income, then, you will see that the total group income amounted to ...
4 ... but what is especially significant is the increase in non-interest income.
5 We've seen the income; let's now look at the outgoings.
6 The accompanying audited financial statements were prepared in conformity with generally accepted accounting principles.
7 This increase is larger than in previous years, and is partly due to ...
8 All this adds up to total group outgoings of ...
9 I think I'll stop there and answer any questions.

B2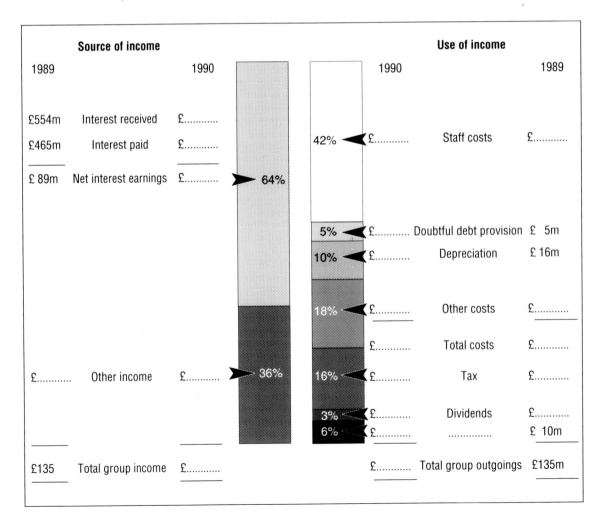

You are going to hear Claire Seal, a merchant banker, giving some information about her bank to a small group of professional visitors from abroad. Before you listen to her presentation, look at these questions. Then listen and answer the questions.

1 In this section is Claire talking about income, costs, or both?
2 Is Claire giving figures with or without comment?
3 Was 1990 a good year or a bad year for the bank?

B3

Look at the diagram below which is a copy of the one which Claire refers to. Listen to her presentation again and fill in the blanks under the heading *Source of income*.

(Note: The blanks under *Use of income* will be filled in in Section C.)

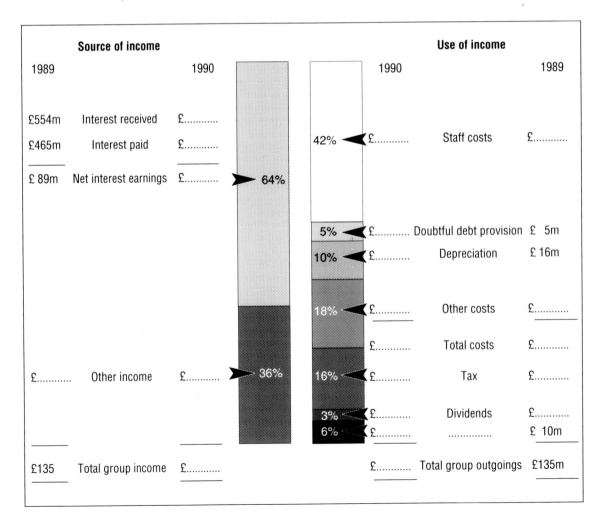

B4 🖭

Listen to the first part of the presentation again. Fill in the spaces in the sentences below with the words actually used.

This diagram gives a very .... of some of the

.... relating to our performance in 1990. We'll be

.... these figures again later in .... ; but it

may be .... at .... to present them and to

.... a number of ....

   If we .... income, ..., you

.... that the total group income .... to a

.... of £150 million, an .... of

.... 15 per cent on the .... year, a ....

.... increase .... above that of recent years.

B5

Choose the one best answer.

1 A *brief summary* is:
   a) a small amount of something; b) several numbers added together to make a total; c) a short report of the main points; d) a full report with details.
2 *Key* figures are:
   a) figures that are easy to understand; b) the most important figures; c) figures that give an answer to a problem; d) figures that are well-known.
3 *Trends* are:
   a) movements or directions; b) goals that you try to reach; c) events that are likely to happen; d) events that happen often.
4 A *record level* of income is:
   a) an amount that will never be reached again; b) an amount that is written down so that it will not be lost or forgotten; c) an amount that stays the same and does not go up or down; d) a higher amount than ever before.
5 *Net interest income* is:
   a) the amount by which the total interest received is higher than the total interest paid during the period; b) the amount by which the total interest received is lower than the total interest paid during the period; c) the total interest received by the lender; d) the amount earned on an investment after paying for its capital cost.
6 Something which is *especially significant* is:
   a) the only one of its kind; b) the very best of its kind; c) important and worth noting; d) widely-known and accepted.

7 *Fee and commission earning activities* are:
  a) the buying and selling of currencies for profit; b) plans to lend money for profit; c) services that are sold by an agent; d) services for which charges can be made.
8 A *contribution* to total income is:
  a) a fixed amount of money paid at regular intervals; b) money that is owed or payable; c) an amount of money that is taken away from the total; d) an amount given or supplied.
9 The *economic environment* is:
  a) an area of the economy; b) the future of the economy; c) the economic situation; d) financial laws and regulations.
10 The *sensitivity of interest rates* is:
  a) the way in which interest rates affect each other; b) the way in which interest rates are easily influenced or affected; c) the changes in interest rates; d) the way in which interest rates are worked out.

Section C C1 🖭

You have heard Claire Seal talk about how much her bank earned last year. Now you are going to hear her talk about how much the bank spent. As you listen to the continuation of the presentation, number the items below in the order in which Claire mentions them.

● Tax   ....
● Provisions for doubtful debts   ....
● Other expenses   ....
● Staff costs   ....
● Dividends   ....

C2 🖭

Look again at the chart in B3 on page 14. Listen again to the continuation of the presentation and fill in the blanks under *Use of income*.

C3 🖭

Look at the following extracts from this part of the presentation. Work with a partner and note down what you think Claire says instead of the words in *italics*. Then listen to the presentation again and compare your answers with the words that she actually uses.

1 ... let's now look at the .... (*amount of money spent*)
2 The largest of these is .... (*money involved in paying employees*)
3 ... to handle the expansion of the bank's .... (*services for which charges can be made*)

4 .... increased to eight million pounds ... (*money put aside to cover possible credit losses*)

5 .... (*the decline in value of property which is hired*) and on .... and equipment ... (*buildings and the land on which they stand*)

6 Other .... increased by ... (*money spent on the running of the bank*)

7 ... the smallest .... increase ... (*yearly*)

8 .... remained unchanged ... (*the part of the company's profits which is paid to shareholders*)

9 ... as the major part of the year's profit was .... (*kept by the company and not paid to shareholders*)

10 Our balance sheet .... (*totals*)

11 After .... of the dividends ... (*setting aside money for*)

12 ... there remained a net .... (*amount of money kept by the company and not paid to shareholders*)

13 ... nine million pounds, which was .... (*moved over to funds put aside to cover unexpected events*)

C4

What factors are important for the financial success of a bank operating internationally? Look through the list of factors below and when you have decided on their relative order of importance, write the number of your choice in column A. Number 1 should show the factor which you consider most important and number 10 the least. You will be told how to fill in column B.

	A	B
Use of advanced technology		
Strong national economy		
Skilled and efficient staff		
Wide range of high quality products		
Broad network of correspondent banks		
Good management		
Wide geographical spread of local representation		
Good market reputation		
Established and diverse customer base		
Other (specify)		

C5

Make a presentation of the recent financial performance of your bank or company to the group or to a partner. Use any visual aids, such as diagrams and charts, to help you. If you do not have these figures, make them up.

Section D   D1

Read the following financial statement from an annual report and then answer the questions which follow.

Wallers Bank plc

Consolidated Profit and Loss Account

31st December 1990

	1990 £000	1989 £000
Profit before tax, after provisions for doubtful debts	24 541	23 863
Tax on group profits	14 395	13 389
Profit after tax	10 146	10 474
Dividends paid	3 250	3 250
Retained earnings	6 896	7 224
Earnings per share	13p	15p

1 What term tells you that this is a statement of income?
2 Do the figures relate only to one bank or to one bank and its subsidiaries?
3 What was the increase in taxable profits from 1989 to 1990?
4 How much more tax did the bank pay in 1990 than in 1989?
5 What is the difference between the 1990 and 1989 figures in terms of the profits which the bank has kept?
6 Are these figures before or after money put aside for possible credit losses?

D2

Look at these questions and answer them when you have read the accounts on the opposite page.

1 Which two specific items on the balance sheet showed the main growth?
2 What was the percentage increase in total assets from 1989 to 1990?

Wallers Bank plc

Consolidated Balance Sheet

31st December 1990

	1990 £000	1989 £000
Assets		
Cash and due from banks	254 095	235 809
Loans to banks and public bodies	1 159 082	998 129
Investment securities	598 820	572 218
Advances to subsidiaries	4 795	3 856
Leased assets	15 867	15 024
Acceptances for customers	530 723	409 820
Premises and equipment	95 415	89 845
	2 658 797	2 324 701
Liabilities		
Current, deposit and other accounts	1 869 952	1 667 153
Deferred taxation	18 052	15 088
Proposed dividends	1 983	1 071
Acceptances for customers	530 723	409 820
Capital Resources		
Share capital	40 000	40 000
Reserves	135 658	128 489
Minority interests	6 687	4 709
Loan capital	55 742	58 371
	2 658 797	2 324 701

D3

Look at the balance sheet again and answer these questions.

1 What term tells you that these figures show the total financial position of the bank at the end of 1990?
2 What is the value of all things owned by the bank which could be used, if necessary, to pay debts?
3 Which sum includes the £5 million which the bank has lent to the City of Birmingham Local Authority?
4 What is the total value of the things such as shares and treasury bills which the bank has bought with the intention of making a profit?
5 What was the increase from 1989 to 1990 in the amount of money which the bank lent to companies which it owns?
6 What is the value of all the property such as buildings, land, motor cars, computers and so on which the bank owns?
7 What is the value of the property which the bank lends to its customers for payment?
8 What is the total value of the debts owed by the bank?
9 Which is greater, and by how much, the taxes which the bank paid in 1990, or the money put aside in 1990 which the bank calculates will soon be needed to pay taxes?
10 If all of the issued shares are paid up and there are 20 million shares at £1 each, how much each did the remaining five million shares cost?
11 How much more money was put aside in 1990 than in 1989 to cover unexpected events?
12 Which term relates to those shares which Wallers do not themselves hold in their own subsidiaries?

D4

Read through the following information.

> Three banks, A, B and C, all issued their financial statements for the 1990 financial year at the same time. In each case, the sum of the retained earnings and dividends adds up to the profit after taxation.
>
> Bank B reported a profit after taxation of £16 million. Half of this sum was paid as dividends.
>
> The bank with total assets of £1.5 billion paid dividends amounting to £5 million.
>
> One of the banks paid dividends which were £1 million higher than those of Bank B. The same bank had total assets which were twice as large as those of Bank A.
>
> Half of Bank A's profit after taxation was kept as retained earnings.
>
> Bank C posted a profit after taxation which was double that reported by Bank A.

Given this information, work out the following:

1 Which bank had total assets of £2 billion?
2 Which bank showed retained earnings of £11 million?

D5

Most of the words in the crossword puzzle are used in Units 1 and 2.

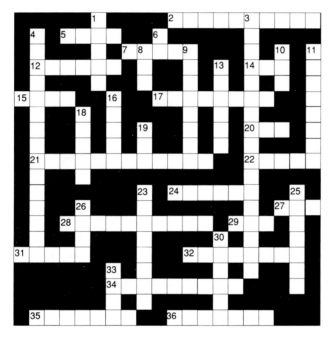

Across

2 Company in which another company owns more than half the shares. (10)
5 Opposite of profit. (4)
7 Periodic examination of financial records. (5)
12 The joining of two or more companies into one. (6)
14 Not the Source of Income, but the ... of Income. (3)
15 A sum of money owed. (4)
17 Buildings and the land on which they stand. (8)
20 Money paid to the government on income. (3)
21 Report detailing a company's activities in the past financial year. (6,6)
22 Interest ... (levels). (5)
24 Not private. (6)
27 After costs and other deductions. (3)
28 Payment as an agreed percentage of price. (10)
29 Very important (figures, etc.). (3)
31 Movement or development. (5)
32 Profits after transfers to reserves. (8)
34 Money overdrawn on a bank account, to an agreed limit. (9)
35 Hiring something to a user, instead of selling it. (7)
36 The total obtained from adding up a column of figures. (7)

Down

1 Something which you own, which can be used to pay a debt. (5)
3 A method of financing international trade. (11,6)
4 Short-term documents normally sold by big US corporations. (10,5)
6 Certificate of deposit. (2)
8 US dollar. (3)
9 The buying of a majority of shares in a company. (8)
10 'Earnings ... share.' (3)
11 Money spent on running a company. (8)
13 Customer. (6)
16 The whole amount, added up. (5)
18 Several companies joined together, owned by one company. (5)
19 Charge made for service. (3)
23 Money put aside in case anything unexpected happens. (8)
25 Sum of money left with a bank. (7)
26 Document promising to pay a sum of money at a specified time. (4)
30 Differences between income and outgoings. (6)
33 A sum of money lent. (4)

D6

Look at the items listed in the *Highlights* shown in A3. Then draw up a similar summary for your own bank or company, based on your most recent profit and loss account and balance sheet. Discuss your summary briefly with another member of the group.

Unit 3 Foreign exchange

Foreign exchange dealing plays an important part in the activities of many banks. In this unit we hear Alan King, the Chief Dealer in a London merchant bank, explain some of the basic principles of foreign exchange dealing. Then we hear him at work on the telephone making two deals.

Section A **A1**

Look through the following list of currency codes. Then write the appropriate currency code next to the country to which it relates in the grid below.

SEK	DEM	CHF	BEF	CAD	USD	GBP	ITL
NLG	NOK	DKK	FRF	JPY	AUD	ESP	

Currency code	Country	Currency code	Country
	Holland		Norway
	Belgium		Sweden
	Great Britain		Denmark
	Australia		Switzerland
	Italy		Germany
	United States of America		France
	Canada		Spain
	Japan		

A2 📼

Listen to Alan King explain some of the basic principles of foreign exchange dealing and tick (✓) those items which he talks about.

1 Currency codes.
2 Some terms used in foreign exchange dealing.
3 Some basic principles of foreign exchange dealing.
4 A big deal he did last week.

A3 📼

Listen to the conversation again. As you do so, note down whether the following statements are true or false.

1 Most of Alan's dealings are based on sterling.
2 The previous day, dollar rates had risen by between ⁄₁§ th to ⁄• th of a per cent.
3 A *tom/next* means from tomorrow to next week.
4 When someone asks 'What is your spot dollar mark outright tomorrow?' Alan quotes them a spot rate.
5 A swap involves borrowing one currency and lending another.
6 An outright is connected to a corresponding spot transaction.
7 This conversation took place in the month of October.

A4 📼

Listen to Alan again and write down the words that he actually uses in place of the words printed in *italics*.

1 We're accounted in *British pounds* ...
2 So, for instance, your *prices for funds which will be exchanged two working days later* are dollar Deutschmark ...
3 I mean, for instance, yesterday the dollar rates *increased slightly*.
4 So people buy dollars because the *difference in interest rates* between dollars and Deutschmarks is *increasing*.
5 You're short of Deutschmarks that day and you have to *buy*, borrow those for one day ...
6 That is the basis of making a *result where the income is higher than the costs*.
7 Well, to *make totals equal, to balance* the account for that day.
8 ... and find that on the 17th that I am *in a position where I have sold more Deutschmarks than I have bought, and bought more dollars than I have sold*.
9 Then you have spot a week, *a period of two weeks beginning two working days from now*.
10 We also have *deals where someone buys one currency and sells another on any particular day*.

11 It's just that you're *stating the price that you will charge for* a spot rate ...

12 ... depending what the price is for the tom/next *exchange of one currency for another, for a certain period of time.*

13 ... so that the relationship between the two currencies *fixes, decides* the forward pricing.

14 ... so they cover their foreign exchange *risk or possibility of loss* by buying Deutschmarks ...

A5 🖳

It is sometimes difficult to hear words which are unstressed in spoken English. Look through the text below, which is taken from the first part of the conversation, and say what you think the missing unstressed words are. Then listen again to this part of the conversation. As you do so, write in the missing words. Then compare your answers with those of a partner.

.... accounted .... sterling, but generally all dealings .... based .... the dollar. So, ... instance, ... spot prices .... dollar Deutschmark, OK? .... the big market really, dollar Deutschmark. And .... the movement in .... dollar which is really moving .... market. I mean, ... instance, yesterday, the dollar rates firmed up .... little. They went up about .... sixteenth to .... eighth of .... per cent. So people buy dollars .... the interest differential between dollars .... Deutschmarks is widening. So .... mean, if you buy dollars, OK, you, you .... lend them out .... next day .... say eleven and .... half per cent. .... short .... Deutschmarks that day, and you have .... purchase, borrow those .... one day, and that's about five .... half per cent. So .... talking about six per cent difference. The basic idea .... spot dealing is to buy dollars low .... sell high. That's the basis .... making .... profit.

Section B   B1

Before you listen to a telephone call, look at the expressions on the next page. Put a tick (✔) by the ones you might expect to hear in a telephone conversation concerning a foreign exchange deal and a cross (✗) by those that you would not expect to hear. Then compare your answers with those of a partner and discuss any differences.

1 In order to confirm the arrangements we made by telephone today, here are the terms and dates on which we agreed.
2 I'm fine thanks. How are you?
3 OK. Just let me get the two week price for you.
4 Hold on for a moment.
5 I can give you two dollars outright.
6 Please advise if 11.00 a.m. on the above date is convenient.
7 Why the dollar will rise again.
8 Nice to hear from you.
9 Just a second.
10 I sold you two million dollars against D marks.
11 Further to our recent telephone conversation, I am enclosing a copy of our tariffs, as requested.
12 Thanks a lot for the deal.

B2

Alan King is calling Tove Strutz, the Cash Manager of a large Scandinavian insurance company. Listen to their conversation and answer these questions.

1 What time of the year does the conversation take place?
2 In this deal does Alan buy Deutschmarks from Tove or sell them to her?

B3

Listen to the telephone conversation again. As you do so, fill in the form below to show Tove's records of the transaction.

CURRENCY PURCHASE/SALE
Bank and dealer
Currency & amount
Rate of exchange
Value date
SEK amount
Date
Notes

B4 🖳

Look at the following expressions. Then listen to the telephone conversation again and write down the words or expressions that are used to mean the following:

1 Actually.
2 Meet each other.
3 Telephone me.
4 State our prices.
5 The price for a currency two working days from now.
6 The price for a currency two working days from now which one bank charges another bank.
7 An exchange rate of Swedish kronor against dollars.
8 The front surface of a computer or terminal on which information is shown.
9 Thousandths of a percentage point.
10 Wait a moment.
11 Available in your account on (date).
12 I agree that we have made a deal.
13 Pay the funds into.
14 Pay the corresponding funds into.

B5 🖳

You are going to hear eight sentences which you might hear in a telephone conversation. Respond to them with one of the sentences shown below.

A OK. Thanks for calling. Bye now.
B Yes, that would be nice.
C Fine thanks. And you?
D Yes, OK. In a couple of weeks, then.
E Let me think. As a matter of fact there is, yes.
F Very well, thanks.
G Yes, that's fine.
H For how much?

Note that not all of these responses actually occur in the section. Some are alternatives which could have been used instead of what was said.

B6

The speakers in this unit all use numbers fluently in their everyday work. But it can sometimes be difficult to know how to say things which we often see written. How would you say the following?

1 $\frac{1}{8} + \frac{3}{32}$
2 $\frac{3}{16}\%$

3 5¾%
4 600, 541
5 2,000,000 dollars
6 7.3980
7 2.6028 ÷ 0.0037 = 2.5991
8 500,000 x 10.64 = 5,320,000
9 240 ÷ 2½ = 96
10 12¼ + 21⅔ = 33¹¹⁄₁₂

Section C C1

1 What, in your opinion, are the essentials for a successful telephone call?
2 What sometimes goes wrong in telephone calls?

C2 ▣

Now listen to Alan King receiving a call from Jan Ackerman, a dealer in the Foreign Exchange department of a Dutch bank, and answer these questions.

1 Is this the first time Alan has talked to Jan?
2 Do they deal dollar/Deutschmark, dollar/pound, or dollar/yen?
3 Is it a big deal or a small deal?

C3 ▣

In quoting rates, note that Alan often specifies only the pips, that is the third and fourth decimal places of the exchange rate. Also, because he does not know whether Jan wants to buy or to sell dollars, he quotes a spread of rates, that is both the rates at which his bank will buy and sell dollars. Now listen carefully to the telephone conversation again and write in below each of the four rates which are quoted.

Spot rate:	Buy $	Sell $
	.... DEM	.... DEM
Two weeks' swap rate:	Bid rate (the bank's lending rate)	Offer rate (the bank's borrowing rate)
	.... DEM	.... DEM

C4 📼

Listen to the telephone conversation again. As you do so, fill in Jan's settlement form.

VAN ZEAHALM BANK
1007 AK Amsterdam

DATE: *November 21*   TO: *Key Commercial*

WE CONFIRM HAVING BOUGHT FROM YOU:

CURRENCY: PURCHASE AMOUNT:

FOR PAYMENT TO OUR RECEIVING AGENTS:

WE CONFIRM HAVING SOLD TO YOU:

CURRENCY: SALE AMOUNT:

FOR PAYMENT TO YOUR RECEIVING AGENTS:

EXCHANGE RATE: VALUE DATE:

C5 📼

Look at the following extracts. Listen to the telephone conversation again and write down in the spaces provided the words that Alan and Jan actually use, instead of the words in *italics*.

1 Good, what's .... , please? (*the exchange rate for dollars against Deutschmarks*)
2 I have probably a small interest in two weeks, ...
   (*lending one currency and borrowing another for a fixed period of time*)
3 OK, ... (*wait a moment*). For two weeks
   .... ? (*beginning two working days from now*)
4 Less than a .... ? (*million dollars*)
5 Can you give me .... ? (*the exchange rate that will actually be used for funds exchanged two working days from now*)
6 OK, I can .... (*sell you half a million dollars in exchange for Deutschmarks*)

7 So two fifty-nine ninety-one is the outright. .... will be
   the ... (*the date on which our money is available in your account and your
   money is available in our account*)

8 Just a second, I've lost my .... (*chart or table showing
   days, months and dates*)

9 .... Thank you very much, Jan. (*We have agreed on the
   sale and purchase of half a million dollars.*)

C6

A dealer at Bank B telephones the Cash Manager at Company C to check on
the company's currency needs. Work in pairs, one person being the dealer
and the other the Cash Manager. See if you can reach a deal. Dealers look on
page 107 for your instructions. Cash Managers look on page 108.

Section D   D1

Read the following report about currency rates and then look at the graphs
below which show the movement of the four currencies during the week in
question. Which graph shows which currency?

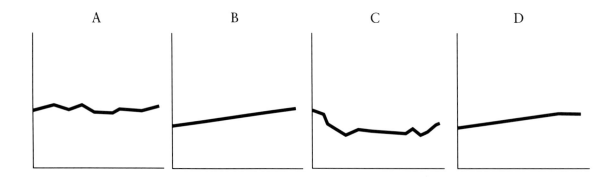

In a quiet week, the US dollar continued its upward course, again trading at nearly three Deutschmarks. The dollar was supported by commercial demand, as normal interbank trading declined and the market's major operators began squaring their positions for the year-end. The forecast of lower US interest rates and of a cut in the Federal Reserve discount rate did not lead to any downturn in the US currency and the dollar closed at DM 2.9925.

The Deutschmark was hardly changed, moving in a narrow range in lack-lustre trading in Frankfurt. There was no central bank intervention to weaken the dollar against the mark. Trading volumes were low as the markets decline towards the end of the year.

Sterling has been volatile lately, due to its status as a petrocurrency, and at the beginning of the week it fell against the dollar and other major currencies, as North Sea oil prices eased on the European spot market. Friday saw a slight recovery, however, due to the covering of short positions, and at close of trading the pound stood at USD 1.3016.

Falls in oil prices have opposite effects on the pound and the yen, as Japan needs to import nearly all its considerable energy requirements. This has meant that the yen has continued its steady climb, levelling slightly towards the end of the week. Against the dollar it has remained little changed since mid-January, but the yen has outperformed European currencies for most of the year. Sterling started the year at around JPY 325, touching a peak of JPY 344 on May 14. It closed on Friday at JPY 337.

D2

Now read the report again and then complete the information below to show the latest currency rates mentioned.

USD 1= ....
GBP 1= ....
GBP 1= ....

On this basis, work out the following cross rates:

USD 1= JPY ....
GBP 1= DM ....

D3

On the basis of the information in the report above, say whether the following statements are true or false.

1 The report was written in mid-January.
2 The dollar firmed up against the Deutschmark during the week.
3 Big banks were more interested in balancing their currency positions than in normal trading.
4 Possible changes in the US interest rates and the discount rate did not affect the dollar rates.
5 The Deutschmark was traded in large amounts in Frankfurt.
6 The exchange rates of the British pound have changed quickly recently.
7 Banks were dealing in sterling on Friday in order to square their currency positions.
8 Falls in oil prices mean that the yen rates go up.
9 The yen rate against the dollar has been roughly the same for eleven months.
10 It is possible to buy more yen with Swiss francs now than it was earlier in the year.

D4

Look at the figures on the next page which show the US dollar currency position of a bank at the close of business on April 14th. On the basis of this information, say whether the bank's total position in US dollars is long or short and if so by how much, or whether the bank has squared its total position.

Accounts in US dollars

A: Position at close of business, April 14th.

Nostro accounts (money placed with foreign banks)	Vostro accounts (deposits received from foreign banks)
USD 50 million	**USD 40 million**
Loans to customers	Deposits from customers
USD 5 million	**USD 10 million**
USD 55 million	**USD 50 million**

B: Forward position in USD.

Forward purchases	Forward sales
Value 21st April	Value 21st April
USD 30 million	**USD 40 million**
Value 29th April	Value 29th April
USD 35 million	**USD 35 million**
USD 65 million	**USD 75 million**

C: Total position.

Unit 4 Meetings

In this unit we will hear extracts from two separate meetings. The first meeting is between a company treasurer and the area representative of an American bank. In the second meeting we will hear the same company treasurer, this time negotiating with a banker from the United Kingdom.

Section A   **A1**

Before you listen to the extract from the first meeting, look at the following expressions. Put a tick (✔) by the ones you might expect to hear in a business meeting and a cross (✗) by those you would not expect to hear. Then compare your answers with those of a partner and discuss any differences. Where would you expect to see or hear those you marked with a cross?

1 One of the points you mentioned in your letter was ...
2 I'm sure we can help you there.
3 Notice is hereby given that the rate of interest for the next interest period has been fixed at nine per cent per annum.
4 Could we take up the question of ...?
5 Perhaps you could consider reducing that?

6 Senior financial managers consult Wallers Bank. Shouldn't you?
7 What kind of reduction did you have in mind?
8 I enclose a copy for your information of the minutes of the meeting held on 23 May 1991.
9 I take your point.
10 OK, I've made a note of it.
11 Applications must be made on the form attached hereto.
12 We'll get back to you within a couple of weeks or so.

A2 🖭

You are going to hear Diane Francis, who is an Assistant Vice-President at the London branch of an American bank, in conversation with Ulf Edberg, the treasurer of Denavian International Insurance. After the meeting, Diane wrote a report on it for her boss. Here, however, the report is not complete. Listen to the conversation and fill in the gaps.

```
Meeting held on ..............................

Location: Denavian Insurance Company, Stockholm

Present: Ulf Edberg (Treasurer, Denavian) - self

Agenda:  1. Letter of Credit Facility

Client is not yet sure about company requirements for

.......................... . Expressed worry, however,

over .......................... and estimates that

this will cost Denavian ................ . Client

pointed out that the countervalue

.......................... is deposited with us.

Currently pays 0.25% for ....................... but

changes will mean .......................... .

Requested that we look into ....................... .

Volume of letters of credit likely to ..............

.............................. .

I promised to ....................... .
```

A3 📼

Listen to the conversation again and write down in the spaces provided the words that Ulf and Diane actually use instead of the words printed in *italics*.

1 One of the points you .... (*referred to or specified*) in your letter was our .... letter of credit facility ... (*present*)
2 ... due to the change in .... (*the law of the United States*)
3 ... I just wonder if we could .... (*look into*) alternatives to the .... (*flexible agreement to provide funds to a third party*)
4 ... at least 0.75 of a per cent per annum .... (*fixed, without variation*)
5 That's on the .... of letters of credit? (*total amount that is owed*)
6 ... what do you call it? – .... with our own securities ... (*an arrangement by which money and other assets are controlled for our advantage*)
7 But I'm sure we will .... the volume of letters of credit ... (*reduce and make smaller*)
8 ... trust funds are something in which we can offer you .... (*a lot of experience, skill and know-how*)
9 I'll go away, give the matter a lot of thought, and give you our .... next month. (*preliminary main suggestions*)

A4

Each of these phrases from the conversation fulfils a particular purpose. Match the items with the definitions.

1 One of the points you mentioned in your letter was ...
2 But I'm worried by the increase in your commissions ...
3 As we discussed last time ...
4 I just wonder if we could explore alternatives to ...
5 I guess we have ...

6 Right.
7 ... a – what do you call it?
8 I think that could be an acceptable alternative ...
9 But I'm sure we will decrease the volume ...
10 So you'd prefer a trust fund ...
11 Fine.

A Agreeing that something is correct.
B Referring to something stated in writing.
C Saying that a course of action is certain.
D Trying to find the right words.
E Saying that you think what you are going to say is correct.
F Expressing concern about charges.
G Suggesting that something is acceptable.
H Agreeing that something is acceptable.
I Referring to a previous discussion.
J Suggesting an alternative.
K Checking that you have understood.

A5

Work in pairs. One person takes the role of Diane, representing the bank and the other takes the role of Ulf, representing the company. Briefly discuss the letter of credit facility offered by the bank to the company. Try to reproduce roughly what Ulf and Diane said.

Section B   B1

Read this letter which concerns the meeting that you will hear in Sections B and C. Here the last paragraph has been left out. Decide which of the alternatives on the next page is the most suitable last paragraph for the letter. Then compare your answer with that of a partner.

Wallers Bank plc

14 Churchgate, London EC2A 2YU
Telephone: 071 586 2314
Facsimile 071 586 2333 Telex: 338539

Mr U Edberg
Denavian Insurance Company Ltd
Kungsgatan 24
111 35 Stockholm
Sweden

6 September 1991

Dear Ulf,

I understand that Mark Grey and I have an appointment to see you at 9.00 a.m. on Tuesday, 24 September, at your offices. We very much appreciate this opportunity and look forward to the meeting.
I thought it would be a good idea to write outlining the topics which we see as being of mutual interest and which we would like to cover during our visit. Principally, these are the following:
  - Our current multi-currency overdraft facility and your company's requirements for 1992.
  - Cash management needs of the company and the bank's capabilities in this area.
  - Long-term funding requirements.
  - UK and North American subsidiaries' requirements.
  - Country risk study.
(*Last paragraph missing*)
Yours sincerely,

Clive Bond

Clive Bond
Director
Commercial Banking Division

Choices for the last paragraph:

1

```
I hope to see you again soon to discuss further points
of co-operation. In the meantime, if you have any
questions or if I can be of any assistance, please do
not hesitate to contact me directly.
```

2

```
Naturally this list is not exhaustive and if there are
any additional topics on which you particularly desire
information or the bank's viewpoint, perhaps you would
let me know by letter or telex.
```

3

```
I trust that the above meets with your approval. I plan
to be in Stockholm toward the latter part of September
and would be delighted to meet with you again to discuss
these matters further, if it is convenient for you.
```

B2

Listen to the first part of the meeting betwen Ulf Edberg and Clive Bond. Then answer these questions.

1 What banking service do Ulf and Clive discuss?
2 What is Ulf's opinion of the charge made for this service?
3 What does Clive promise to do?

B3

Here are Clive's incomplete notes of his meeting with Ulf. Listen to the conversation again and complete the notes.

Client raised the question of the .... Says that 1% over

.... is too expensive.

Wants us to reduce our margin to .... Stated that with

Key Commercial, Denavian pays only .... Client pointed

out that in a recent credit rating Denavian was rated .... for

short-term debt and .... was rated ....

I promised to .... I feel that if we do not reduce our

margin, it is very unlikely that ....

B4

Look at the words in the box, all of which are from this section. Check any words that you do not know with a partner. Then, working together, match the words with the correct definition from the list below.

confirm	overdraft facility	mark-up
credit rating	review	margin
overnight rate	LIBOR	quite frankly
credit committee		

1 A banking service providing for borrowing on current account up to an agreed maximum limit.
2 The rate of interest charged for a loan at call from one day to another.
3 The gross profit margin or an increase in price.
4 Honestly and directly, without wishing to hide anything.
5 London Inter-Bank Offered Rate, the rate of interest between London banks on some deposits.
6 The relation between profit and selling price.
7 A group of bank staff who control the lending of the bank.
8 A formal and detailed examination of the financial strength of a company.
9 To look at or examine again.
10 To give agreement.

B5

You are going to hear seven sentences taken from the meeting you have just listened to. Say something appropriate in reply to each of them, choosing from the list below.

A I see.
B Yes, do that.
C Yes, certainly.
D OK, I've made a note of that.
E Yes, we feel that's about right.
F It's our basic lending rate, which is 12 per cent just now.
G Well, say 0.25 per cent above your base rate.

Note that not all these replies actually occur in the section. Some are alternatives which could have been said instead.

B6

Work in pairs. One person takes the part of Ulf, the other of Clive. Discuss the interest rate charged on the overdraft facility. Try to reproduce roughly what they said.

Section C   C1 🖭

Listen to the second part of the meeting between Ulf and Clive.

1 What does Ulf want?
2 What does Clive agree to do?
3 What is Ulf's view of his company's relationship with the bank?

C2 🖭

Listen to the discussion again. As you do so, make brief notes for Clive as a basis for the report which he wrote later. Then compare your notes with those of a partner and discuss any differences. Finally, with your partner write a short report based on your joint notes.

C3 🖭

Listen to the discussion again and write down in the spaces provided the words that Ulf and Clive actually use instead of the words in *italics*.

1 I see that we've got .... (*the bank's services for the safe keeping of our securities*) on the .... (*list of business to be discussed*)
2 ... we've checked up on the charges for this, and really it comes to .... (*a very large sum*)
3 So now we have started to .... with the different banks ... (*discuss and try to come to an agreement*)
4 ... we pay £200 per fixed rate .... (*business deal involving investments such as stocks, shares and bonds*)
5 ... and £50 per .... (*ordinary shares deal*), plus a .... (*fixed sum for services*)
6 ... that would cost us the .... of one million Swedish kronor ... (*same amount as*)
7 So in that case your .... seem out of line ... (*charges for certain services*)
8 Yes, not all of that eight billion is with us of course, but I .... (*see what you mean*)
9 .... , I was interested in ... (*in general*)
10 ... everything can usually be .... over the phone. (*discussed and put right*)
11 It's only that a couple of .... should be made ... (*changes to make things more suitable*)
12 Otherwise, no .... (*negative statements expressing dissatisfaction*)

C4

Which of the qualities listed below do you think are most important for someone to be successful in negotiations? Put them in order of importance, 1 to 8 and then compare your ideas with those of a partner.

- Flexibility
- Calmness and self-control
- Friendliness
- Ability to analyse situations
- Reliability
- Well prepared with information
- Ability to communicate
- Other (*Please specify.*)

C5

Read the following information.

> Bank B provides services for Company C. Principally, these are as follows:
>
> 1 Standby letter of credit. The charge is ¾% on the outstanding volume. The average outstanding volume last year was £400,000.
>
> 2 Overdraft facility, with a limit of £2 million. The charge is Bank B's base rate (10%) plus ¾%. The average overdrawn amount last year was £500,000.
>
> 3 Custodian services. Company C pays £50 per equity transaction. Last year there were 550 such transactions.

Work in pairs, one person representing Bank B and the other representing Company C. If you represent Bank B, look on page 107 for your instructions. If you represent Company C, look on page 108. Negotiate terms in accordance with your instructions.

Section D   D1

On the next page is the follow-up letter Clive sent to Ulf soon after their meeting. The last paragraph has been left out. Decide which of the alternatives on page 43 is the most suitable last paragraph for this letter. Then compare your answer with that of a partner. Discuss your choices, if they are different.

Wallers **B**ank *plc*

14 Churchgate, London EC2A 2YU
Telephone: 071 586 2314
Facsimile 071 586 2333 Telex: 338539

Mr U Edberg
Denavian International Insurance Company Ltd
Kungsgatan 24
111 35 Stockholm

2 October 1991

Dear Ulf,

Although Mark Grey is currently on a business trip to
the Middle East, he certainly joins me in thanking you
and Carola for what was not only a most enjoyable but
also a very informative and useful meeting during our
recent visit to Stockholm. Thank you also for the
excellent dinner which you provided. It is always a
pleasure visiting Stockholm and I hope that when you are
next in London you will allow us to return your
hospitality.

(*Last paragraph missing*)

With best wishes,

Yours sincerely,

Clive Bond
Director
Commercial Banking Division

Choices for last paragraph:

1

> In addition o the material enclosed, we will send you
> shortly information on trust funds, with a comparison of
> costs between trust funds and standby letters of credit.

2

> We hope that our meeting will serve to strengthen our
> relationship with Denavian. We are giving serious
> thought to all the issues you raised and can assure you
> that the needs of Denavian will be well attended to.

3

> We are following up on the several matters discussed
> which require action and I will be writing to you more
> fully in due course. Meanwhile, thank you once again for
> your generous time and the very enjoyable dinner.

D2

Look at the document on the next two pages which refers to the overdraft facility discussed by Ulf and Clive in Section B. Then answer these questions.

1 Place a tick (✔)next to those currencies which are available under the terms of this facility.
   a) Japanese yen
   b) Swiss franc
   c) British pound
   d) Deutschmark
   e) Polish zloty
2 When and for what periods will Denavian pay any interest charges due under this facility?
3 How will Denavian pay any such interest charges?
4 What must Denavian obtain in order to be able to use this facility?
5 What legal system applies to the agreement?
6 For how long is the facility available?
7 Who has to sign the agreement on behalf of Denavian?

Wallers Bank plc

14 Churchgate, London EC2A 2YU
Telephone: 01 586 2314
Facsimile 071 586 2333 Telex: 338539

Our ref: AC/MB/LB
 14 May 1991
Denavian International Insurance Company Ltd
111 35 Stockholm
Sweden

For the attention of Mr Ulf Edberg

Dear Sirs,

 Multi-currency (except sterling) Overdraft Facility for USD 10,000,000.00

Further to your letter of 20 April 1991, we are pleased to advise you that we are willing to place the above-mentioned facility at your disposal on the following terms and conditions:

Limit: Up to USD 10,000,000.00 (say ten million United States Dollars) or equivalent outstanding at any one time.

Purpose: To provide working capital.

Availability: Drawings may be made in major currencies (subject to availability), except sterling.

Charges: Interest will be charged at the rate of 1% over Wallers' Base Rate. Such interest will be calculated on a day to day basis and debited to your account quarterly in arrears at the end of March, June, September and December.

Exchange Control: This facility is granted subject to the approval of the Central Bank of Sweden.

Jurisdiction clause: This facility letter shall be governed and interpreted in all respects in accordance with English law and you accordingly submit to the jurisdiction of the High Court of Justice, London. It shall be open to us to enforce repayment in the Courts of any competent jurisdiction.

Validity: This facility is available until further notice, but is subject to review by us not later than 14 October 1991.

Please signify your acceptance of these terms and conditions at your earliest convenience, by signing the attached copy of this letter in accordance with your

Authorised Signature list and returning it to us. Please
enclose the relevant approval from the Central Bank of
Sweden.

Yours faithfully,
For and on behalf of Wallers Bank Limited

Clive Bond

We accept the terms and conditions specified above.

For and on behalf of Denavian International Insurance
Company Limited,

Signed ....
Date ....

D3

Look through the following information.

Three banks, A, B and C, all provide services for the same big company.

Only one bank provides a trust fund instead of a standby letter of credit facility. Bank A charges ½% on the outstanding volume of letters of credit.

Each bank provides only one overdraft facility and only one of these facilities is multi-currency. The other two are sterling. There is a £2 million limit on the overdraft facility provided by Bank C.

Bank A holds securities worth £4 million in a custodian account for the company, which is twice the value of securities held in the company's custodian account by Bank C. The bank which provides a trust fund does not provide the company with custodian services. The same bank does, however, provide the company with an overdraft facility with a limit of £5 million.

Given this information, work out the following:

1 Which bank charges the company ¼% on the outstanding volume of standby letters of credit?
2 Which bank has a limit of $10 million on the company's overdraft facility?

D4

Most of the words in the crossword puzzle are used in Units 3 and 4

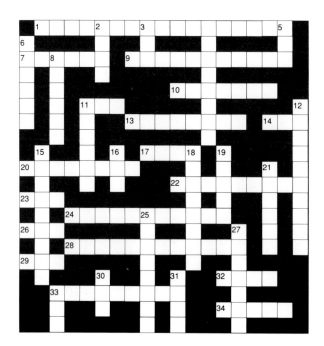

Across

1 A service for borrowing on current account up to an agreed limit. (9,8)
7 Relation between profit and selling price. (6)
9 Laws. (11)
10 Give agreement. (7)
11 Public limited company. (3)
13 Buy. (8)
14 US dollar. (3)
17 Exchange one currency for another for an agreed period. (4)
20 Deal where you buy one currency and sell another. (8)
22 Fourteen days. (9)
23 French franc. (3)
24 Charges as an agreed percentage of price or volume. (11)
26 Belgian franc. (3)
28 Same value. (7,5)
29 Dutch guilder. (3)
32 Thousandths of a percentage point. (4)
33 Price for funds which can be exchanged two working days later. (4,5)
34 Conditions of an agreement. (5)

Down

2 'I agree we have just made a deal.' (4)
3 Charge made for a service. (3)
4 Chart or table showing days, months and dates. (8)
5 Japanese currency unit. (3)
6 Sum. (6)
8 Look at or examine again. (6)
11 Difference between income and outgoings. (6)
12 A change, to make something more suitable. (10)
15 Happening every three months. (9)
16 Swiss franc. (3)
18 Suggestion. (8)
19 Exchange ... are the values of currencies in relation to each. (5)
21 List of business to be discussed. (6)
25 Name given to the British pound. (8)
27 Charged and deducted. (7)
30 Italian lire. (3)
31 Nought. (4)
33 Swedish krona. (3)

D5

Write a letter to Mary Choyto who works for a bank in Hong Kong. You have spoken to her on the phone once, but have never met her. Suggest a meeting with her during your four-day visit to Hong Kong next month and mention two alternative times. Specify the items that you would like to talk about.

Unit 5 A Presentation

In this unit we will hear three parts of a presentation about currency options by John Morley. He is Executive Director of the foreign exchange division of a London merchant bank and is making his presentation to a group of cash managers and treasurers from different corporate clients.

Section A   **A1**

Here are the steps which John uses in planning his presentation strategy. Choose the five steps which you think are the most important for the making of a successful presentation in their order of importance and then discuss your choices with a partner.

1 Set the objective of the presentation.
2 Research the topic.
3 Analyze the needs of the audience.
4 Formulate a clear introduction.
5 Select information which the audience needs on the topic and which makes the advantages clear.
6 Review the advantages and finish with a clear closing statement.
7 Provide time for audience questions.
8 Include language techniques to help direct the attention of the audience.
9 Prepare visual aids.
10 Practise the entire presentation.

A2

Before you listen to the first part of the presentation, look at the following expressions. Put a tick (✓) by the ones you might expect to hear in a presentation concerning currency options and a cross (✗) by those you would not expect to hear. Where would you expect to hear or read those marked with a cross? Compare your answers with those of a partner and discuss any differences.

1 I would like to say first of all thank you for coming.
2 Claims as aforesaid must be received not later than 30 days after the expiry of the guarantee.
3 Perhaps we could begin by outlining ...
4 First of all, what is a currency option anyway?
5 We now have to look at why the option has a particular place for the commercial user.
6 Wallers Bank announces that, with effect from 30 October 1991, its base rate is decreased from 12% to 11.5% per annum.
7 So here are a number of situations described so far where you actually have something that is providing some unique advantages.
8 I attach a proposed agenda for this year's conference.
9 If we get down to something a little bit more practical ...
10 What can I get you?
11 I'd like now to draw the main threads together.

A3 🖭

Listen to the beginning of John Morley's presentation. As you do so, make brief notes on what John says. Some headings are given here to help you.

Currency options market:

Forward contracts:

Treasury services:

Leadership position:

Medium-size to large companies:

A4

Listen to this part of the presentation again and say if these statements are true or false.

1 John begins by introducing himself and by thanking his listeners for coming.
2 John says that currency options are quite complicated.
3 There will be opportunities later for discussion with subject experts.
4 John expects currency options to become as important as forward contracts.
5 John's bank was one of the first to introduce all kinds of new services in the currency options field.
6 John believes that his bank does as much currency options business as any other bank in the world.
7 John expects the retail banks eventually to do larger volumes in currency options business than his own bank.
8 John does not expect larger banks to have the same tailor-made element in currency options services as his own bank will have.

A5

John uses several phrases that are useful when beginning a presentation, some of which are given in the list below. Look through these phrases and plan the introduction to a talk about a banking service that you know about. Use as many of the phrases from the list as you can in any order that you choose. Then make your presentation.

> And the idea is to ...
> One of the areas which ...
> Good morning. I'm ...
> Perhaps we could begin by ...
> I would like to say first of all ...
> ... and this is intended to be an opportunity for you to ...
> We have got a number of services in ...

Section B   B1

John Morley continues his presentation. Which of these items does he talk about?

● The history of currency options.
● What a currency option is.
● Currencies available.
● Advantages of currency options.
● Options and treasury services.

B2

Here are the incomplete notes John used in this part of the presentation.
Listen again and then complete the notes so that they are similar to the slide
he used.

Option buyer has the right to

_____

But no obligation to do so.
Option writer has the right to
_____ *at the*

price demanded.

B3

Complete the currency flow diagrams below by writing the events in the
appropriate boxes. Listen again to this part of the presentation if necessary.

1 Foreign Currency Call Option

Events
Receives base currency.
Delivers specified currency.
Receives specified currency.
Delivers base currency.

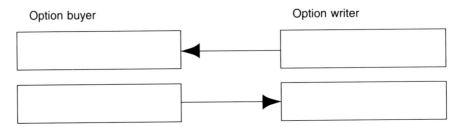

Option buyer   Option writer

2 Foreign Currency Put Option

Events
Receives specified currency.
Receives base currency.
Delivers base currency.
Delivers specified currency.

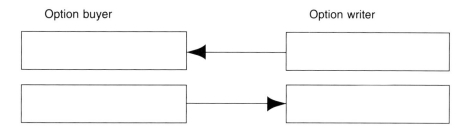

Option buyer   Option writer

B4

Below is a slide which John uses to describe the advantages that are offered by currency options. The list here, however, is out of order. Specify the two advantages to which John refers in this section in order. Listen again to this part of the presentation if necessary.

Advantages
- Known worst case
- Range of strike prices
- Cover downside; keep upside
- Profit lock
- Contingent cash flows

B5

Choose the best answer.

1 If you *purchase* something:
   a) you hire it; b) you deliver it; c) you buy it; d) you state how much it costs.
2 An *obligation* is:
   a) something you must do because there is a legal or moral requirement to do it; b) a particular thing that you want to do; c) a document promising to pay a sum of money; d) a sum of money owed by one person to another.
3 *Value spot* is:
   a) a period of two weeks beginning two working days from now;
   b) the price for funds which will be exchanged two working days from now; c) the price for a currency in terms of the currency of another country; d) the date two days ahead on which funds are available in the bank.
4 Something that is *straightforward*:
   a) happens immediately without delay; b) happens too quickly; c) is simple and uncomplicated; d) is very serious and important.

5 Anything that is *unique* about the option is:
a) to be found only in the option; b) to be found mainly in the option;
c) difficult to understand; d) new and not very well known.

6 A *deal* is:
a) a business agreement; b) a business relationship; c) a way of saving
money; d) a person who buys and sells things.

7 A *principal* advantage is:
a) an advantage that you believe in; b) a general advantage; c) an
advantage in theory but not in practice; d) a main advantage.

8 *Downside risk* is:
a) the possibility of a fall in value; b) the possibility of a rise in value;
c) the possibility of a fall in quality; d) the possibility of fewer
advantages.

9 If something happens *simultaneously*, it:
a) happens without being planned; b) happens before something else;
c) happens after something else; d) happens at the same time as something
else.

10 A *premium* (here) is:
a) a large sum of money; b) a sum of money set aside for a particular
purpose; c) a charge for the use of an option; d) a demand for payment.

B6

Each of these phrases from the presentation fulfils a particular purpose.
Match the items with the definitions.

1 First of all, what is a currency option anyway? What are we talking about?

2 Can everyone see that?

3 Like an ordinary foreign exchange deal.

4 So that's the essence of it.

5 It's a perfectly straightforward initial idea.

6 We now have to look at why the option has …

7 What is it that's unique about the option that gives it certain advantages that make it the best deal?

8 … and we'll come and discuss some of them in more detail.

9 A principal advantage is that …

10   An option does that.

A Stating a feature of something which makes it better than anything else.

B Saying that you are going to talk about something later.

C Saying that something is simple.

D Moving on to the next point.

E Making a comparison.

F Emphasizing that an option fulfils a function already referred to.

G Introducing a definition or explanation.

H Introducing the main feature of something which makes it better than anything else.

I Checking that everyone can see an illustration.

J Saying that you have spoken about the main features of something.

B7

Now plan a short introduction about a product with which you work, or if you prefer, about currency options. Try to use as many of the phrases in B6 as you can in any order you choose. Then make your presentation.

Section C   C1 🖅

Look again at the slide shown in B4. Listen to the third part of John Morley's presentation and number the remaining advantages to show the order in which he mentions them in his presentation.

C2 🖅

Listen to this part of the presentation again. As you do so, make brief notes. The headings you have numbered 3, 4 and 5 on the slide will help you. Then compare your notes with those of a partner and discuss any differences.

C3 🖅

Listen to this part of the presentation again and write down in the spaces provided the words that John actually uses instead of the words in *italics*.

1 An option is .... useful for covering contingent cash flows ... (*especially*)
2 .... , for instance, where you might get the order ... (*written offers to supply goods or carry out work at a stated price*)
3 Range of .... (*exchange rates agreed for a currency option*)
4 You can't .... to deal at some other rate. (*choose*)
5 Most companies reckon they can live with a few cents .... of an exchange rate. (*movement*)
6 So you can .... , depending on ... (*change the charges that you pay for the use of an option*)
7 ... by which I mean that if you are .... , for instance, and the dollar has been going up and up ... (*in a position where you have bought more dollars than you have sold*)
8 You can take out an option to sell the dollars at .... (*today's price*)
9 ... if it goes up, you effectively you have locked in that amount of .... (*financial gain or advantage*)
10 And .... might find this profit lock effect a useful one. (*people responsible for a company's money*)
11 ... an option and obtain .... which you cannot get any other way. (*an advantage*)

C4

A good speaker uses language to help direct the attention of the listeners. Look at some of the techniques below which a speaker can use to focus the listener's attention on important points.

- Enumerate: The first point is …
- Emphasize: A principal advantage is …
- Repeat: … a 15 per cent rise in costs. 15 per cent!
- Restate: Let's look at that another way.
- Focus: Look at these figures.
- Link: We've seen the advantages; let's now examine the costs.
- Explain: Finally, profit lock, by which I mean …
- Sum up: So here are a number of situations described so far where …

Now prepare a short presentation about a service or a product with which you are involved. Try to include each of the eight techniques above, in any order, though not necessarily using the same words. Your audience will make notes while they listen to your presentation.

Section D   D1

1 Read the letter from John Morley to one of the guests who was at his presentation. The letter contains nine paragraphs. Read it quickly and match the ideas below with the appropriate paragraph number.

A Stating the price of a service.
B Specifying terms and conditions.
C Offering a facility.
D Offering to state the price of a specific service.
E Generally inviting business and offering service.
F Saying who should use a service and when.
G General introduction of a service.
H Explaining how a service works.
I Stating the purpose of writing.

Wallers **B**ank *plc*

14 Churchgate, London EC2A 2YU
Telephone: 071 586 2314
Facsimile 071 586 2333 Telex: 338539

Wilhelm Haussmann
Corporate Finance Director
GVZ AG
Quai de Vendome
8007 Zurich
Switzerland

18 March 1991

para.

1

Dear Wilhelm,

It was a pleasure to see you at the bank on March 7 and 8. During our Thursday afternoon meeting, we briefly discussed several points and, as promised, we are now writing to you concerning the three major issues raised.

2

Firstly, we noted your interest in learning more about our interest arbitrage operation, a service by means of which we are able to provide very attractive interest rates in all major currencies. The way in which these loans are arranged is by the use of sterling bills of exchange, so-called 'eligible bills', which can be discounted in the London discount market. This market reflects the short-term (one to six months) domestic interest rate level in the United Kingdom and often provides cheaper funding than LIBOR-related instruments.

3

Companies to whom this form of lending will appeal are, in particular, those that have a borrowing requirement in a currency in which they have receivables available for repayment at the end of the loan period. According to the regulations of the Bank of England, the bills must support a commercial transaction such as export, import or domestic trade.

4

We arrive at our interest rate through discounting sterling bills on behalf of our customer and converting the net proceeds into the required currency at the spot rate. Wallers then enters into a forward contract with the customer for the purchase of the currency to be repaid at maturity of the loan and all the rates used for these transactions combine to produce the interest rate quoted to the customer (see Appendix 1 for example).

5   Secondly, you expressed interest in opening a Sterling Current Account and I am now pleased to be able to offer you this facility on the following terms and conditions.

6   For your requirements in Sterling we would operate a current account in your name, transacting all standard banking items and paying interest on any cleared credit balances as follows:

- Up to £25,000   - Nil
- £25,000 to £100,000   - Wallers Call Rate less 1% p.a.
- Over £100,000   - Wallers Call Rate (currently 9% p.a.)

I enclose a copy of our standard charges for standard items, but would operate the account free of charge for say six months, except for:

- Clearing bank telex charge for same day value payment to one of their branches
- Special clearance costs
- Daily telex statement charge

After six months, we would review the arrangement in the light of account activity, balances held and prevailing interest rates.

7   We can provide a daily Telex Statement of Account which would be available to you each morning, itemizing all the transactions of the previous day and including the opening and closing balances. Our fee for this service is £600.00 for each account.

8   Finally, you mentioned your forthcoming negotiations for the takeover of a United States company. The exchange risk that arises for you as a contingent liability during the negotiations is clearly a considerable one and one that is best covered, for reasons already discussed, by the use of a currency option. We would be particularly pleased to take this matter further, by advising you as to an appropriate strike price and by quoting a very competitive premium.

9   We thank you for giving us the opportunity to assist you with your banking requirements and look forward to setting up an active and growing relationship with your group of companies. Meanwhile, if you have any queries, please do not hesitate to contact me.

```
With best wishes,

Yours sincerely,
```

[signature: John Morley]

```
John Morley
Executive Director
Foreign Exchange Division
```

2 What are the three main topics of the letter?

D2

Look at these steps describing the bank's interest arbitrage system and number them in the order you think they happen.

- Bills are discounted in the London discount market.
- Bank enters into a forward exchange contract with the customer.
- Bank accepts sterling bills from customer.
- An overall interest rate is calculated on the basis of all the other rates.
- The loan matures and the customer repays the agreed currency amount.
- Net proceeds are exchanged for the currency required at the spot rate.

Now compare your sequence with that in the letter.

D3

Write a letter to a new customer, describing a service offered by your bank or company.

Unit 6 Trade finance

Banks play an important role in the financing of international trade. In this unit we will hear about the financing provided by one bank and then we will listen to two bankers meeting to discuss matters of trade finance between their two banks.

Section A **A1**

What are your country's main exports? What are your country's main imports? Who are your main trading partners? Discuss these questions with a partner.

A2

Look through the survey below. To which countries do you think a foreign bank would most be prepared to finance the exports of one of its customers? List the countries in order of preference for the bank, with number 1 as the best country to export to and number 5 as the worst. Then compare your order with that of a partner and discuss any differences.

Payments Survey

Country	Usual terms	Payment situation	General situation
Eastland	Normal range of terms. Increasing requests for longer credit terms.	Some delays reported. Amounts under USD 3,000 processed faster.	Steady economic growth should continue. Downward import trend forecast.
Southlasia	Documentary credits commonly used.	Strict exchange controls. Prior approval of Central Bank necessary for all import settlements.	Rigid import controls: licences issued only for priority categories. Politics unsettled.
Northland	Normal market terms. Currency normally USD or ECU.	Generally satisfactory.	Business conditions favourable. General election next year.
Newlandia	Normal terms apply.	Good payment record. FX easily obtained for payments abroad.	Politically stable. Enormous FX reserves, despite reduced oil revenues.
Westina	Fully secured terms advised.	Customer default and slow payments affecting suppliers. Caution required.	Rocketing inflation. Tough budget in June. Acute shortage of FX.

A3 🖳

Roy Meadows and Christine Stannard, who work in the international trade and banking division of a British clearing bank, are explaining their trade finance services to a potential customer, Peter Baker. Listen to their conversation and answer these two questions.

1 Does Roy talk about trade finance in broad terms or does he go into detail?
2 Does Christine give an example about the past, the present or the future?

A4 📼

Before he met Roy, Peter listed some of the points he wanted to ask about.
Listen to the conversation again and tick those points that Roy and Christine
cover.

- Experience in helping large companies?   - Advice?   - Import licences?
- Bank's services covering our exchange risk?   - Export factoring?
- Documentary credits?   - Documentary collections?
- Banks and agent's abroad?   - Forfeiting?

A5 📼

Listen to the conversation again and write down in the spaces provided the
words that Roy and Christine actually use in place of the words in *italics*.

1 ... involved with the very large .... (*British companies*)
2 ... involved in international trade, the .... (*companies
   operating in several countries*)
3 ... these large corporates, plus their .... (*the companies in
   which more than half the share-capital is owned by one of these
   corporates*)
4 ... a .... export order to France. (*possible but not yet actual*)

5 ... and the .... (*legal agreement*) was originally drawn in
   .... (*British pounds*)
6 ... because they are not permitted to .... (*buy foreign
   currency in advance so as to protect against changes in the exchange
   rates*)
7 ... the necessary sterling to pay the .... (*invoice, the list of
   charges to be paid*)
8 So we got some .... (*statements of price*)
9 ... . back to the customer. (*with no right of demand*)
10 ... all sorts of .... (*arrangements between a bank and an
    importer by which the bank pays the foreign exporter as soon as certain
    conditions have been met*)
11 ... whether they should be .... (*cannot be cancelled
    without the agreement of all parties*)
12 ... whether they should be .... (*include an undertaking by
    the paying bank that it will pay the amount due if the issuing bank does
    not pay*)
13 ... we deal with .... and so on. (*arrangements under which
    the importer must first pay before the bank will hand over the documents
    that he needs in order to get the goods*)

Section B **B1**

1 Look at the following article and suggest the best headline from this list.

Good news for foreign investors

Fall in profits

Setback for growth

Trade deficit increases

A recent .... (1) by the Southlasia Statistics Institute predicts that the economy will .... (2) by a mere 0.1 per cent this year, in contrast with the two per cent estimated by the government. The Institute also .... (3) a continued trade .... (4), higher inflation and rising unemployment. To .... (5) the decline in the country's foreign exchange reserves, the government has introduced .... (6) measures to curb imports, and has .... (7) several joint .... (8) development contracts. Southlasia's external debts .... (9) total the equivalent of three years of the country's exports at 1991 .... (10).

2 Now fill the spaces with suitable words from the box.

stringent	deficit	postponed
currently	halt	profit
forecasts	grow	venture
levels	study	capital

B2

Look at the following extracts from a business meeting. Put a tick (✔) by the ones you might expect to hear in a business meeting and a (✗) cross by those you would not expect to hear. Where would you expect to see or hear those you marked with a cross? Compare your answers with those of a partner and discuss any differences.

1 Accounts maintained by each Bank in connection herewith shall constitute prima facie evidence of sums owing to such Bank hereunder.
2 OK, I see.
3 We were wondering if this sum could be increased.
4 I'm sorry, I'm afraid we can't.
5 These instructions will remain in force until advised otherwise by the undersigned.
6 We'd be very pleased if you could consider ...
7 Another point I'd like to bring up is ...
8 I can't say offhand.

9 It is mutually agreed between the parties hereto as follows ...
10 OK, that about concludes my list of points.
11 Just to sum up the situation ...
12 I think we've covered everything now, haven't we?
13 It was good of you to see me.
14 For the conditions on which credit is to be opened, see overleaf.
15 Thank you for coming in.

B3 📼

Kai Larsen, whom we met in Unit 1, is meeting Ken Chiswanda who works for a Southlasian bank. As you listen to their conversation, decide if the meeting is to discuss:

1 routine matters
2 specific problems
3 a new proposal

B4 📼

Listen to the meeting again. As you do so, make brief notes under the following headings. Then compare your notes with those of a partner and discuss any differences. What do you think of the suggested solution(s) and why? Can you offer a better solution?

> Kai's points
>
> Ken's points
>
> Suggested solution (s)

B5 📼

Listen to the meeting again and write down in the spaces provided the words that Ken and Kai use in place of the words in *italics*.

1 Our banks have had .... for eight years ... (*an agency arrangement with each other*)
2 ... and whether you have any questions about the ....
... (*way in which things work*)
3 Yes, we have one .... (*topic which is more important to us than any other*)
4 ... even though the credits are payable, in fact, ...
(*immediately they are received*)

5 We .... of course by paying market-rate interest ... (*make you a suitable payment for loss*)

6 ... the .... laid down by our Central Bank. (*fixed ways of working*)

7 ... but then to be able to .... we need the permission of ... (*meet a liability, to pay as we promised*)

8 ... an import .... from the Ministry ... (*official permission in writing*)

9 ... the goods have been examined .... shipment ... (*before*)

10 They ended the .... (*situation in which only one company has the right to provide a service*)

11 ... and .... (*as a result*) during the .... traders stockpiled shipments. (*time between two events*)

12 ... all arrived in Southlasia at the same time, causing a .... (*lot of work which is late and still waiting to be done*)

13 But unfortunately we're still left with .... (*an amount which is less than the required amount*)

14 ... the 950,000 Swiss francs that are .... (*not yet paid*)

15 I'll then check things up and try to .... for you. (*make things go faster*)

B6

Match the phrases in the left-hand column with the purpose in the right-hand column.

1 I was interested to know how you see the ...

2 Yes, we have one main point of concern, certainly ...

3 Over the last year we've noticed that ...

4 ... I think it's fair to say ...

5 OK, I see. But unfortunately ...

6 I believe we ...

7 I can't say offhand.

8 What I'd like to ask you to do, if I may, is to ...

A Saying that you need to check on information before you can give an answer.

B Stating an observation made on the basis of experience.

C Making a polite request for action.

D Asking for a person's point of view.

E Indicating that you are not absolutely sure what you are saying is correct.

F Indicating that what you are saying is reasonable.

G Saying that there is a fact or situation which worries you.

H Expressing understanding and a regret.

B7

Work in pairs, one person representing Bank A, the other Bank B. With your partner select one of the problems from the list below for discussion.

Representative of Bank A: Raise a problem about your business with Bank B.

Representative of Bank B: Offer explanations and propose a solution.

In your discussion of the problem, try to use as many of the phrases from B6 as you can.

Problems

● There is an average delay in payment of confirmed documentary credits by Bank B of 30 days.
● One documentary credit issued by Bank B for USD 650,000 has not been paid, even though it is now three months overdue.
● Documentation sent by Bank B concerning documentary credits is very often inadequate. There always seems to be something missing.

Section C   C1

Look at the terms in the left-hand column and match them with the definitions in the right-hand column.

1 line	A	Payments that are owing and overdue.
2 utilized	B	Definite.
3 concrete	C	Rules are followed.
4 beneficiary	D	Receipt from the ship's master for goods received for shipment.
5 confirming bank	E	A person named to receive payment.
6 prohibit	F	Pay the money that is owing.
7 domestic politics	G	Income from oil rises and falls often.
8 oil receipts fluctuate	H	The political situation in a country.
9 federal authorities	I	Document sent by exporter to importer recording sale of goods.
10 relevant licence	J	Government organizations.
11 honour debts	K	Make impossible and prevent.
12 delays in reimbursement	L	Document stating the country in which goods have been manufactured.
13 arrears	M	A sum of money available to draw on.
14 regulations are complied with	N	Used.
15 commercial invoice	O	Lateness/slowdown in being paid back money spent as agent.
16 bill of lading	P	The bank which guarantees payment if the issuing bank does not pay under a documentary letter of credit.
17 certificate of origin	Q	Necessary official written permission.

C2 🖭

Ken and Kai continue their meeting. How many points do they discuss? Can you say what the points are?

C3 🖭

Listen to this part of the meeting again. As you do so, make brief notes under the headings given here.

Proposals

Response

Concluding points

C4

Read this information.

Bank A has a correspondent relationship with Bank Z, and representatives of the two banks now have a routine annual meeting. Bank A is in an industrialized country with strong economic growth. Bank Z is in a politically unsettled country with falling oil revenues and a shortage of foreign exchange.

Bank A has established a line of credit for Bank Z for confirmation of credits of up to $2 million. Bank A at present experiences an average delay of 40 days in the payment of confirmed documentary credits by Bank Z. No interest is paid. Three credits totalling £95,000 have been outstanding for seven weeks.

Work in pairs, one person representing Bank A and the other Bank Z. If you represent Bank A, look on page 108 for your instructions. If you represent Bank Z, look on page 107. Try to reach broad agreement in accordance with the instructions you are given.

Section D **D1**

First read this letter which concerns a documentary credit issued by Ken's bank in Southlasia.

METROPOLITAN AND PROVINCIAL BANK PLC

100 Corporation Street
Birmingham B1 2PS

Morley Knight Ltd.
21 Paradise St
Warrington

Our ref: LBS 1504

1 May 1991

Dear Sirs,

We have been requested by Abbotville Bank, Southlasia, to advise you of the issue of their irrevocable credit number DW1924 in your favour for account of Hoglund Trading Co Ltd., Box 5504, Furness, Southlasia, for GBP 22,629 (say pounds sterling twenty-two thousand six hundred and twenty-nine) available by your drafts on Metropolitan and Provincial Bank PLC at 60 days sight accompanied by the documents specified below:

1. Invoice in quadruplicate, indicating LC no. PWH77YL.
2. Full set clean on board bills of lading, marked 'Freight Prepaid' and 'Notify Hoglund Trading Co Ltd., Box 5504, Furness, Southlasia'.
3. Packing list in triplicate.
   4. Insurance certificate in duplicate.

Covering:
"5 PCS ENGINE MODEL PV-37 AS PER PURCHASE ORDER NO. 322/IP7 DATED 15 APRIL 199" (All of which must be stated on your invoice.)
Shipment from Warrington to Furness c.i.f. not later than 30 June 1991.
Partial shipment not permitted.
Transhipment not permitted.

Drafts drawn under this Credit must be presented not later than 30 June 1991.

We are requested by our principals to add our confirmation to this Credit. Accordingly, we undertake to honour all drafts drawn under and in strict conformity with the terms of the Credit, provided that such drafts bear the date and number of the credit, and that the credit and any amendments thereto are attached.

We are instructed to claim our charges in connection
with this credit from your good selves.

Yours faithfully,

CA Slattery

A. Slattery
Manager

Now look through the extract from a blank documentary credit form below.
What information did this part of the form contain when it was received
from Southlasia by the Metropolitan and Provincial Bank? Look through the
above letter again and then write in the relevant information on the form.

NAME OF ISSUING BANK	IRREVOCABLE DOCUMENTARY CREDIT
	Number:
	Date:
APPLICANT	**BENEFICIARY**
ADVISING BANK	**AMOUNT**
	Partial shipments allowed ☐ not allowed ☐
Shipment/dispatch from	Transhipment allowed ☐ not allowed ☐
For transportation to	Date of expiry

We have issued the documentary credit as detailed below. We request you to
notify the said credit to the beneficiary

☐ without adding your confirmation.   ☐ adding your confirmation.

D2

Look at the letter again and then answer the questions on the next page.

1 How many copies of each of the following does the bank request from the exporter?
   a) invoices
   b) bills of lading
   c) packing lists
   d) insurance certificates
2 When is the contract sum to be paid to the exporter?
3 Exactly what is Hoglund Trading Company buying from Morley Knight?
4 Who pays for the shipment and insurance costs of the order, and how?
5 How many shipments does the deal involve?
6 Can the shipment be transferred from a British ship to a Southlasian ship during the journey?
7 How many weeks does the exporter have in which to present drafts for payment under this credit?
8 What must the drafts include when they are presented for payment?
9 Other than the documents mentioned in Question 1 above, is there anything else that should be sent with the drafts when they are presented for payment?
10 Who pays the advising bank's charges in connection with this credit?

D3

There was a six month delay in reimbursement from the issuing bank to the Metropolitan and Provincial Bank concerning this credit. Write a short letter from the Metropolitan and Provincial Bank to the bank in Southlasia, briefly detailing the situation and claiming for the loss of interest on the credit for the time period in question. Specify the interest rate you are claiming and the amount, as well as the dates on which you paid the credit and on which you received reimbursement. Request immediate settlement of your claim.

D4

Look through this information.

Bank X has a correspondent relationship with three foreign banks, A, B and C.

The Bank experiences a delay of 30 days in the payment of confirmed documentary credits by Bank A and a delay of 50 days in the case of Bank C.

The Bank provides Bank A with a line for confirmation of credits up to $2 million. It provides the bank which pays confirmed documentary credits at sight with a line for confirmation of credits up to $3 million.

Bank X also provides one of the banks with a line for confirmation of credits up to $1 million, and the economy of the latter bank's country depends on exports of coal. The bank which pays confirmed documentary credits at sight is in a country where the national economy depends on exports of machinery.

Given this information, which of Bank X's correspondent banks:

1 pays confirmed documentary credits at sight?
2 has a line for confirmation of credits up to $1 million?
3 is in a country where the economy depends on oil revenues?

D5

Most of the words in the crossword puzzle are used in Units 5 and 6.

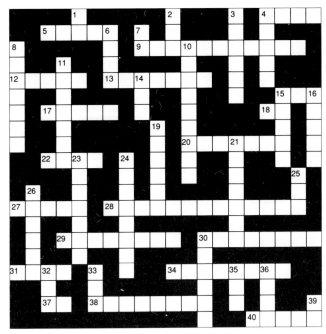

Down

1 Per annum. (2)
2 After costs and other deductions. (3)
3 To meet a claim when due. (6)
4 Movement, change. (5)
6 Control, keep within fixed limits. (4)
7 Short for number. (2)
8 Most of us have one of these with a bank, where we place our money. (7)
10 An amount less than the required amount. (9)
11 Official permission in writing. (7)
14 Cost, insurance, freight. (3)
15 Very serious. (5)
16 Sums of money that are owed. (5)
19 Difference between income and outgings. (6)
21 A bill to be paid, concerning the sale of goods or services. (7)
23 Money owing and overdue. (7)
24 Date on which a note or loan becomes due for payment. (8)
25 A source of energy, an important export for some countries. (3)
26 Government plan for future national income and spending. (6)
30 Written offer to supply goods or carry out work at a stated price. (6)
32 European Currency Unit. (3)
33 British pounds. (3)
35 Pieces. (3)
36 A sum of money available to draw on. (4)
39 Foreign exchange. (2)

Across

4 For immediate delivery. (4)
5 Swiss currency unit. (5)
9 Remaining to be paid. (11)
12 Request something that is due by right. (5)
13 A lot of work that is late, still waiting to be done. (7)
15 Put together with something else. (3)
17 Lateness in something happening. (5)
18 Letter of credit. (2)
20 Payable immediately. (2,5)
22 Business transaction. (4)
27 State a selling price. (5)
28 Operating in several countries. (13)
29 Make impossible, prevent. (8)
30 Department responsible for managing a company's funds. (8)
31 A matter to be dealt with. (4)
34 Situation in which only one company has the right to operate. (8)
37 United Kingdom. (2)
38 Buy. (8)
40 Message sent by electronic machine. (5)

Unit 7 Financial news

Every day important financial news is being made somewhere in the world. This unit contains news items about companies and markets. Each section deals with a different area of business and relates to a different day.

Section A   **A1**

Look through this short news report and then fill the spaces with words from the box.

The dollar opened .... (1) in London yesterday, having .... (2) back sharply in the Far East overnight. During the day, however, it .... (3) its losses against most leading .... (4), with the .... (5) of sterling, which held its ground and closed almost a cent .... (6) at 1.4385 (1.4295). Sterling also .... (7) over one pfennig to 3.7900 (3.7785) against the Deutschmark.

ahead	currencies	weaker
firmed	exception	slipped
fell	recovered	business

A2 📼

Listen to the beginning of the news report. Say if the dollar had:

● a bad day
● a good day
● a quiet day, neither good nor bad

A3 📼

Listen to what the newscaster says about the survey concerning trading on the world's foreign exchanges. Then complete the chart below by showing the amount traded in the leading centre and naming the three leading centres.

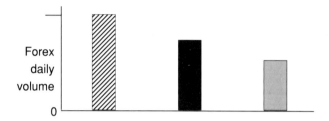

A4 📼

Listen to the third part of the news report again and then complete the grid to show the different dollar rates that are given.

London close of business yesterday	New York close of business yesterday	Tokyo close of business today	London this morning
DEM	DEM	JPY	DEM

A5 📼

Listen to the final part of the news report concerning the latest currency prices in London. Then circle the right alternative in the table to show the actual currency rates given.

GBP	USD	USD	USD	USD	USD
USD	DEM	CHF	FRF	NLG	JPY
1.54.5	216.38	2.16.6	8.14	2.79.5	215.85
1.44.5	263.8	2.60.6	8.40	2.97.5	250.58

A6

Choose the one best answer.

1 If prices *drifted down* they:
a) fell heavily; b) fell slightly; c) fell quickly; d) rose then fell.

2 A *survey* is:
a) a report based on inspection; b) a document that describes what is expected in the future; c) a detailed description of goods; d) an official list of things or events.

3 *Forex volume* is:
a) a sum of money that is borrowed; b) a sum of money that is invested; c) the volume of money in a country; d) the volume of foreign exchange.

4 If *trading was thin*:
a) buying and selling was not very successful; b) there was a lot of buying and selling; c) there was not much buying or selling; d) there was no buying or selling at all.

5 *US economic indicators* are:
a) the index of retail prices produced by the US government; b) figures that show the difference between the amount of money flowing into and out of the USA; c) figures dealing with economic activities in the USA; d) the total amount of money that other countries owe to the USA.

6 *US consumer prices* are:
a) a list of prices to be paid for goods imported into the USA; b) the index of retail prices produced by the US government; c) the prices charged for goods exported from the USA; d) the prices charged for US dollars expressed in the money unit of another country.

7 *Durable goods orders* are:
a) orders for goods which are intended to be used over a period of time;
b) orders for goods which are used up soon after they are bought;
c) orders for any type of goods; d) orders for goods to be exported.

8 If information is *released*, it:
a) is for sale; b) is kept secret from the public; c) is made known to the public; d) is written down and recorded.

9 A *gain* is:
a) a change in value; b) an increase in value; c) a fall in value; d) a value that stays the same.

10 If the dollar *slipped back a little*, it:
a) fell slightly; b) fell unexpectedly; c) fell quickly; d) rose then fell.

11 *The covering of short positions* is:
a) banks buying a currency because they had previously sold more than they had bought; b) banks selling a currency because they had previously bought more than they had sold; c) banks buying and selling currencies so as to make a profit; d) banks buying a currency and selling it soon.

12 If the pound was *aided by firmer* spot oil prices, it was:
a) helped by higher spot oil prices; b) not helped by higher spot oil prices; c) helped by lower spot oil prices; d) not helped by lower spot oil prices.

A7

What have been the main currency movements recently, and why? Give any figures that you can.

Section B   ## B1

Read this short financial news report and then replace the words in *italics* with suitable words from the box.

Share prices again closed higher in *active* (1) trading on the Northland Stock Exchange, based on a firm domestic bond market and hopes of a *drop* (2) in interest rates here and in the USA. *Prospects* (3) of lower interest rates aided *gains* (4) for banks in general, with Quintorp Bank leading the way with a $1.69 *rise* (5).

Major (6) electrical stocks were *somewhat* (7) lower, with the MacOng Corporation *easing* (8) $1.05. Industrial issues closed *broadly* (9) higher, with blue-chip issues showing the most volume and the largest gains.

In other market news, prices closed higher in Tokyo and Sydney, *mixed* (10) in London and Milan and lower in Frankfurt, Paris and Zurich.

varied	slightly	
falling	increase	fall
the possibility	range	leading
busy	generally	advances

B2

Listen to the part of the news report relating to companies and stock markets.

1 How many firms are mentioned in the company headlines?
2 How many stock markets are mentioned?

B3

Listen to the part of the report again and say if these statements are true or false.

1 Lewhill employs around 1,500 people.
2 Welby Engines have obtained a £30 million order from Air Texas.
3 Basterfield's bid for Garvin has been turned down.
4 London stock market prices yesterday reached record highs.
5 Sheldon have sold their interest in Quinton.
6 The price of leading stocks rose slightly on Wall Street on Tuesday.

7 On Wall Street on Tuesday more stocks rose than fell in price.
8 Hong Kong shares showed a heavier fall than Tokyo shares.
9 Shares in general fell sharply in Australia.
10 Many shares were sold in Australia.

B4 🖾

Listen to the part about company news and the London stock market, and look at the following charts which show the quarterly profits for three companies mentioned. Complete the grid below to show which chart relates to which company.

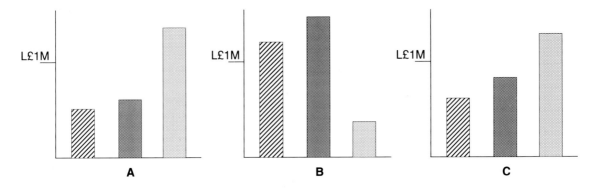

Company	Chart
Hale and Owen	
Fisher Hogg	
Luxdon	

B5 🖾

Listen to the part of the news report which gives information on yesterday's stock market prices in London. Then complete the table below.

Company	Price £	+ or -
United Alverson		
Key Commerce		
Ainscough and Lee		
Sheldon		
Hale and Owen		
Berry Sugar		

B6

Write down the words that the newscaster actually uses in place of the words in *italics*. If you need to, listen to the news items again.

1 Lewhill is to open .... in Birmingham. (*a factory costing £30 million*)

2 Welby Engines have .... a £25 million order ... (*succeeded in obtaining*)

3 ... and the latest .... (*price offered*) for Basterfields by the .... (*very large Canadian company*) Garvin has been .... (*decided against*)

4 .... , (*In the area of news dealing with the outcome of a company's trading during only part of the year*) Luxdon's third quarter profit of £300,000 came as a .... (*disappointment and difficulty*)

5 ... with a 50 per cent profits rise compared with .... (*the last period of three months*)

6 ... . remained close to last week's record highs. (*the parts into which the ownership of a company is divided*)

7 .... (*finance companies and finance organizations which buy and sell bills of exchange*) were .... (*an area of business activity tending to rise*)

8 ... Ainscough and Lee were up nine at 437 on .... (*hopes of an offer to buy*)

9 ... on their Monday sale of their .... (*financial interests in Quinton*)

10 ... which in fact .... (*hide a difficulty*), if one .... (*does not take into consideration*) the .... (*money obtained*) from the .... (*arrangement by which they sold their head offices in Birmingham on condition that they were then hired back to them at an agreed rent*)

11 ... on .... (*uncertainty*) about the .... (*price of the raw material*)

12 On Wall Street on Tuesday .... (*major shares were slightly higher in price*)

13 .... were strong. (*documents promising to pay sums of money at specified times*)

14 In Australia, ... (*all share prices moved downwards suddenly*) although .... (*there was not a lot of buying and selling*)

Section C   **C1**

Look through this short news report about commodities and fill the spaces with words from the box.

> Commodities trading was quiet yesterday, with .... (1) low and price .... (2) narrow. Copper .... (3) within a £2 price range, and ended the day .... (4). Only tin among .... (5) showed any life, gaining £5 a tonne. Lead, aluminium and zinc all .... (6).
> .... (7) commodities were similarly quiet. Coffee prices were .... (8) unchanged, and cocoa prices dropped back a few pounds. Sugar traded mixed, ... (9) fresh developments.

awaiting	fell
traded	ranges
volumes	charges
virtually	soft
metals	down

C2 🎧

Work with a partner and write a brief list of commodities that are traded. Then, as you listen to the commodities news, tick the ones that are mentioned. Are there any mentioned that you did not list?

C3 🎧

Listen to the first part of the commodities news again and then fill in the grid below to show the different prices of gold at the times and places given.

London opening yesterday	London closing yesterday	New York opening yesterday	New York closing yesterday	Hong Kong opening today	Hong Kong closing yesterday

C4 🎧

Then listen to what is said about silver prices and fill in the grid below.

London silver prices
Spot price, previous close
Spot price, today's close
Three months price

C5 📼

Listen again to the information given about base metal prices and fill in the grid below.

Base metal	London settlement prices yesterday
	8,473
Nickel	
	958
Aluminium	
	420
	271.5

C6 📼

Read the three following summaries and then listen again to the details that the speaker gives about these commodities. Say which one of the three summaries is most accurate.

1 Cocoa fell and coffee was strong. Raw sugar fell and sugar futures also fell late in the day. In New York cotton prices were slightly lower and in Chicago grain futures were lower, although November wheat was up three quarters at 225⇔¢.
2 Cocoa climbed after its recent fall and coffee prices were high. Raw sugar and sugar futures both fell. In New York, cotton prices were slightly lower and in Chicago grain futures too were mainly slightly lower.
3 Cocoa climbed after its recent fall and coffee was strong. Raw sugar fell, although sugar futures were steady. In New York cotton prices were unchanged and in Chicago grain futures were mainly slightly lower.

C7

Write down the words that the newscaster actually uses in place of the words in *italics*. If you need to, listen to the news items again.

1 In the London .... yesterday ... (*market dealing with bars of gold and silver*)
2 New York gold prices were .... up 20 cents ... (*very slightly higher, slowly moving*)
3 ... with .... at 428 pence ... (*the price which is to be paid for delivery two working days from now*)
4 ... and .... at 438.5. (*the price which is to be paid for delivery three months from now*)

5 .... were little changed ... (*prices in New York for the delivery of silver on a specific date at an agreed price*)

6 .... (*certain common metals*) drifted lower in reaction to ....(*the stronger British pound*)

7 Among the .... (*non-metal commodities*), cocoa .... after its recent fall ... (*recovered*)

8 .... were steady, but then ... (*contract prices for the delivery of sugar on a specific date*)

9 In New York, cotton .... (*prices were slightly lower*)

10 ... though .... was up three quarters ... (*the price for corn to be delivered in December*)

C8

What has been in the financial news over the last week or so? Take what you consider to be the most important two or three events and describe them in more detail.

Section D   D1

Quickly read the following newspaper article and then choose what you think is the most suitable headline from this list:

> **Bank prices fall**
>
> **Financial problems for two US corporations**
>
> **Bad winter for RJC Bank?**
>
> **Chairman resigns**
>
> **Latin American debt problem**

The international banking community showed signs of worry last week over rumours that RJC Bank, America's tenth largest bank, was close to bankruptcy, acquisition or a forced merger, due to a severe liquidity crisis. The concern underlines the nervousness of the major international banks with regard to loans to developing countries, especially those in Latin America. In the case of RJC Bank, the problem is added to by bad domestic loans, particularly to the depressed energy sector.

At the end of 1988, RJC had $29.9 billion in deposits, making it number ten in the US banking league. Since then, things have gone very badly.

On the New York Stock Exchange, RJC shares have fallen from a 1989 high of $44.25 to an all-time low of $10, reached last Tuesday. This means that the capitalization of the group has crashed from $1.8 billion to some $420 million over an 18 month period. On Friday, however, when Wall Street stock prices generally eased in thin trading, investors showed some confidence in RJC's future, whose share price rose $1.275 to $12.075 by close of business.

The previous chairman of RJC, Lee Dobbs, resigned earlier this year amid rows over the bank's lending, and one of the first moves of the new chairman and chief executive, Jim Kent, was to try to improve the capital base of the bank by selling certain assets. Its credit card business was sold in May to Key Commerce for some $1 billion.

At the company's annual general meeting early last month, Kent told shareholders that non-performing loans, up by $450 million in the first half, would cost over $40 million this year if they neither rose nor fell. Over half the $450 million rise to $2.1 billion stemmed from Latin American credits, notably to Westina, where the bank advanced some $210 million in 1989, as a package designed to meet the country's external financing needs. The status of this loan, and the bank's other outstanding loans in the area, must be regarded as questionable. Approximately 56 per cent of the bank's loan portfolio is outside the United States.

But the bank's latest problems have occurred closer to home. At the end of last month, the Brown McCoy Corporation defaulted on a $9 million repayment on a loan provided by five banks, including RJC. In an attempt to prevent the bankruptcy of Brown McCoy, its banks are now planning to lend it a further $80 million.

Only this week another RJC borrower, Thomas Ainscough Corporation, an Austin-based oil group, filed for reorganization under the US bankruptcy code. The corporation has unsecured loans totalling $210 million, of which $40 million is outstanding to RJC.

In 1990 RJC's net credit losses rose to $269 million from $140.3 million in 1989. If the pattern continues over the second half of 1991, it could be a cold winter for RJC.

D2

Look at this list of events which are mentioned in the article. Number them in the order in which they actually happened. Then compare your answers with those of a partner and discuss any differences.

... Jim Kent appointed chief executive of RJC Bank.
... RJC share prices reach a high of $44.25.
... Thomas Ainscough Corporation files for reorganization.
... Annual General Meeting of RJC Bank.
... Lee Dobbs resigns as chairman of RJC Bank.
... RJC sells its credit card business for $1 billion.
... RJC shares reach their lowest ever rate of $10.
... Brown McCoy Corporation defaults on a $9 million repayment.
... RJC share prices climb $1.275 to reach $12.075.

D3

On the basis of the information in the article, say whether these statements are true or false.

1 At the end of 1988, there were nine US banks with total deposits of more than 29.9 million dollars.
2 RJC Bank has approximately 42 million shares.
3 RJC Bank's share price when the New York Stock Exchange opened last Friday was $10.80.
4 Net credit losses will rise by $40 million this year.
5 At the end of 1990, the bank had non-performing loans totalling $1.6 billion.
6 44% of the bank's lending is to domestic customers.
7 The article was written in early 1991.
8 The bank's net credit losses rose by $128.7 million last year.

D4

Look at the article in D1 again and briefly list the main point of each paragraph. Then read the following three summaries of the article. Say which summary is best and why.

1

RJC Bank, the tenth biggest bank in the USA, with deposits of nearly $30 billion, is in serious financial difficulty. On Wall Street, the bank's share prices have fallen to approximately one quarter of their levels a year and a half ago.

The previous chairman resigned recently, over the bank's loans. Over half of the bank's total volume of lending is outside the USA. Non-performing loans amount to over $2 billion, and Latin American loans in particular could cost the bank a lot of money. Bad loans in the USA are also causing problems for the bank. One corporate customer which owes the bank $40 million is itself in a serious financial situation.

The bank's net credit losses nearly doubled last year. If the same thing happens this year, the bank will face very big problems indeed.

2 | America's tenth biggest bank, RJC Bank, is in financial trouble because of its loans to Latin American countries and to the weak energy sector at home.

Non-performing loans rose by $450 million last year, and will cost the bank $40 million this year. Over half of these loans are to Latin America and include $210 million advanced to Westina in 1989. More than half of the bank's outstanding loans are to Latin America.

Two big loans in the USA have also caused problems recently. One company has failed to repay $9 million to a group of five banks which includes RJC Bank. The banks are now planning to lend the corporation $80 million more, to try to get it out of trouble. Another customer owes $210 million, without security, and is filing for reorganization under US law.

The bank's shares have fallen sharply over the last eighteen months, and net credit losses have risen from $140 million in 1989 to $269 million in 1990. RJC Bank could be in for big trouble.

3 | The financial position of RJC Bank has become serious over the last 18 months. The bank's share prices have fallen heavily during this time, and the chairman resigned earlier this year after angry arguments about the bank's lending.

Non-performing loans have risen by $410 million during the first half of this year, and over half of this rise comes from Latin American credits. If non-performing loans remain as they are, they will cost the bank around $40 million this year. Some 56 per cent of the bank's total lending is outside the USA.

Domestic loans are also causing problems, however, as shown by two recent cases. The first involves lending, with four other banks, a further $80 million to help save a corporation which has already failed to repay $9 million. The second involves a $40 million loan without security to a company which has $170 million outstanding in other loans.

Net credit losses rose by around 90% last year. If this goes on during the second half of 1991, then the position of the bank could become even more serious than now.

D5

Work in small groups to plan and present a particular item of financial news. Your teacher will give you more information.

Unit 8 Projects

Many projects involve very large sums of money and financing these projects is often undertaken internationally with co-operation between several banks and government agencies. This unit is about such financing.

Section A **A1**

What large projects are being financed, or have recently been financed, in your country? Alternatively, what large projects has your bank been involved in financing in recent years?

A2

1 Look at the newspaper report and choose the best headline for it from this list.

International co-operation

Mixed credits for Eastland

Consultant gives go-ahead

Nuclear power for Eastland

An Anglo-Swedish .... (1) has .... (2) a contract worth about $1.5 billion to build a nuclear power plant in Eastland. The .... (3), the Eastland State Power Authority, asked all .... (4) to submit comprehensive financing .... (5), which were then evaluated by the German consultant, Becker-Bungert. The Anglo-Swedish bid was the only one to contain a mixed credit .... (6).

The consortium, led by Strutz of Stockholm, has the .... (7) of the Swedish and British governments, who have both arranged packages consisting of 60 per cent export credits and 40 per cent aid. The aid is at 3.5 per cent over 25 years and the export credits, at the .... (8) consensus rate of 10.5 per cent, are for ten years.

2 Fill in the spaces with appropriate words from the box.

current	proposals	package
costs	consortium	backing
won	client	bidders

A3 🖳

Roy Meadows is explaining project-related banking services to Della Tyson, a trainee at the bank. Listen to their conversation and answer these questions.

1 Is Roy talking about finance offered mainly by a British government department or mainly by British banks?
2 Does Roy's illustration refer to a short-term, medium-term or long-term loan?

A4 📼

Here is a list of items that Della made to ask Roy about. Listen to the conversation again and tick those items that Roy mentions.

- finance of civil engineering projects
- exports of multinational companies
- export of capital goods
- export of semi-capital goods
- buyer credits
- syndicated loans
- front-end loans
- package deals

A5 📼

Listen to the conversation again and say whether these statements are true or false.

1 The Export Guarantee Department is run by the Department of Trade.
2 ECGD-supported finance covers major civil engineering projects and large export contracts.
3 The bank and the ECGD together cover up to 85 per cent of the contract value.
4 The front-end loan to the exporter is for 100 per cent of his export price.
5 85 per cent of this type of loan is repaid over a period of five years.
6 Roy gives only one example of a package deal.
7 The exporter has to pay a premium to the ECGD for this type of financing.
8 Roy says that most buyer credits are either in dollars or Deutschmarks.
9 This type of financing can include cover against any changes that might occur in exchange rates between the time of tendering and the award of the contract.

A6

Fill the spaces on the next page with appropriate words or phrases from the box.

tendering	award	quote
major civil engineering projects	packages	credit
exchange rate fluctuations	commissions	purchase
preferential fixed rate of interest	instalments	outset
an additional premium	front-end loan	to enable
capital and semi-capital equipment	recourse	
progress payments	contractors	
balance of payments difficulties		

1 .... can perhaps lead us to ... (*agreements combining several matters*)
2 This is an area which covers .... (*very large construction works*)
3 ... and the export of .... (*goods that are made to be used to make other goods*)
4 ... . and machinery, that sort of thing. (*industrial equipment, tools*)
5 ... where .... is offered over five years. (*the lending of money*)
6 ... currency problems, ... difficulties and so on. (*difference between the country's total payments to other countries and the total revenue received from them*)
7 ... . the buyer in that country ... (*to make it possible*)
8 ... back to the UK, for the .... (*buying*)
9 ... through what we call a .... (*loan given so that part payment can be made at the beginning of a contract*)
10 ... that is paid at the .... , upon shipment of the goods ... (*beginning*)
11 ... the 85 per cent can be paid in .... (*a series of regular part payments*)
12 ... and .... (*payments for the completion of certain work*) are made to the .... (*companies who are doing the construction work*)
13 ... and the only .... to the exporter is if ... (*right to make a demand on*)
14 The buyer is charged a .... set by ... (*rate of interest which is agreed and which does not change, and which is more favourable than the general market rate*)
15 ... as well as certain .... which ... (*charges for a service, often in the form of a percentage of the sum involved*)
16 ... which ECGD will .... on a case to case basis. (*state the price that they would charge*)
17 ... to pay .... (*an extra amount for a service*) to cover against any .... (*continual changes in exchange rates*)
18 ... between the time of .... (*offering to supply goods or services at a stated price*) and the .... of the contract. (*giving*)

A7

With a partner, compare the government services which help large export orders from or imports to your country with the one which you have just heard about.

Section B   **B1**

Look through this survey from a trade magazine and answer these questions.

1 How many loans involve import/export and how many involve projects?
2 Which is the smallest loan?
3 Which loan is for the longest period?
4 In how many cases are interest rates specified?
5 How many loans are provided by one bank only?

Syndicated loans survey

Borrower	Project	Value	Terms	Bank
Newlandia Petroleum Corporation	Buyer credit to finance supply of drilling equipment.	GBP 25.75m	Two tranches: first in 2 yrs, bullet repayment; second repayable in 28 quarterly instalments. Rates not available.	Sole provider: Key Commercial
Tokig Industries	To finance export of capital goods.	JPY 2bn	6 yr maturity. First yr is drawn down period. Amounts outstanding then rolled into a 5 yr term loan.	Lead manager: Cybulski Corp
Cockle Development Company	Construction of hotel/shopping complex.	DEM 80.5m	8 yrs at 7⁄16% over 6 mth LIBOR.	Lead managers: Siddons Int, ZB Bank
Government of Northland	Hydro power station.	CHF 150m	Swiss bond rate plus margin. 20 yrs.	Lead manager and agent: RJC Bank
Newlandia Transport Authority	Supply of vehicles to Newlandia.	USD 10m	Eurodollar loan. 7 yrs at 10.5% fixed rate. 1 yr 3 mths grace.	Sole provider: Wallers

B2 🖭

Ken Bailey, the Executive Director of a London merchant bank, is being interviewed about his work.

1 Is Ken explaining how his bank finances projects or discussing a project financed by his bank?
2 How many questions does the interviewer ask?

B3 📼

Look at the following stages in the arrangement of a syndicated loan by Ken's bank. Put them in the correct order of events. Then listen again to the interview and check your answers.

A Appointed as lead manager.
B Maintain contacts.
C Decide whether or not to finance it solely themselves.
D Advisory conversations with the customer.
E Send offer document to other banks.
F Compete with other banks.

B4

Write down the words that are actually used in place of the words in *italics*. If you need to, listen to the interview again.

1 As a .... (*bank which is mainly concerned with the financing of international trade*) we .... for corporate customers ... (*provide services only*)

2 ... longer term finance than a ....? (*bank which is a member of a central organization through which cheques are presented for payment*)

3 ... the main method for .... in recent years ... (*arranging loans for long periods of time*)

4 ... mainly to large .... worldwide ... (*organizations set up for specific purposes*)

5 ... by arranging a .... (*sale of bonds in dollars or some European currencies by a group of banks*)

6 ... who are likely to .... in that borrowing (*take part in*)

7 So that's where the .... of long-term money ... (*original starting point*)

8 And then as .... in a loan ... (*an organizer of the other banks*)

9 ... hydro-electric company, say, ... in Africa ... (*arranging the buying of machinery and equipment*)

10 ... hopefully you'd be .... the lead manager. (*given the job as*)

11 ... you may have .... (*enough money*)

12 ... if there are ten issues .... being sold ... (*at present*)

13 ... adding say a sixteenth to the .... (*income received from an investment*)

8 The total value of goods and services produced by a country in a

B5 🖭

By stressing different words in a sentence, we can indicate different meanings. Here are seven short extracts from the conversation between Ken and the interviewer. Each is followed by two statements that might be understood from the speaker's words. Listen carefully to how Ken actually says these words and decide which meaning is intended.

1 As a merchant bank we cater solely for corporate customers ...
   a) ... and only for corporate customers.
   b) ... and other types of bank cater for other customers.
2 The method, the main method for raising long-term funds in recent years
   ...
   a) ... although there are also other, less important methods.
   b) ... although earlier, things were different.
3 So that's where the source of long-term money has come ...
   a) ... and not from anywhere else.
   b) ... but short-term money has come from other sources.
4 You would then decide whether you wanted to finance the whole of it
   yourself ...
   a) ... and not before.
   b) ... or just part of it.
5 So the customer probably wouldn't have a direct contact with those other
   banks ...
   a) ... but our bank would have direct contact.
   b) ... because all his contact is with us.
6 We would have a lot of advisory conversations with the customer ...
   a) ... too many conversations, in fact.
   b) ... in order to make the situation quite clear for the customer.
7 We would advise our customer to wait ...
   a) ... but we cannot stop him if he wants to go ahead.
   b) ... and not to do anything just now.

● Which words would you stress in the sentences above to give them the alternative meanings? Decide with a partner. Then read each of the sentences in one of the two ways for your partner to say whether you mean a) or b) in each case.

Section C   C1 🖭

Ken Bailey receives a phone call from Paul Black, a civil servant in Northland. Listen to their conversation and answer these two questions.

1 Is this the first time that Ken and Paul have discussed the project?
2 Does Ken give a firm answer?

C2 📼

Below is a copy of the form which Ken fills in as a record of important telephone calls. Listen to the phone conversation again and fill in the form for Ken.

TELEPHONE MEMO

Subject:

Client:

Contact person: *Paul Black*

Project:

Sum:

Action required:

Signed:

Date: *2 January – 1991*

C3

Check the meaning of the words and phrases in the box with a partner. Then, working together, match the words with the correct definition from the list below.

economic indicators	treasury department	joint venture
senior civil servant	quarter	trade balance
lead manager	GNP	terms
civil engineering work	documentation	established
participants	in the black	
raising a large sum of money	turnkey basis	

1 A top person in one of the departments of national government.
2 The government department that controls the finances of a country.
3 Organizing the obtaining of a lot of money.
4 The planning and construction of buildings and roads and suchlike, usually for a government.
5 A partnership, in this case temporary, of two or more companies to co-operate on a specific project.
6 A contract arrangement whereby the contractor completes the whole project and then hands everything over to the client, ready for operation.
7 Figures dealing with economic activity which give a general idea of changes in the economic climate.

particular year.
9 A fourth of a year.
10 The difference in the value of imports and exports of a country.
11 In credit, without debt.
12 Those who take part in an activity.
13 The principal party co-ordinating a syndicated loan.
14 Made certain of the fact.
15 Rules or conditions.
16 The papers relating to a business deal.

C4

Look through this list of telephone techniques and decide what you think is their order of importance to the success of business telephone calls. Then compare your opinions with those of a partner.

Find out the other side's needs.
Avoid arguments.
Involve the other person in the conversation.
Use the other person's name in the conversation.
Ask frequent questions.
Check understanding, by summarizing points of agreement.
Plan the call in advance.
Keep a record of important calls.
Give necessary information.
Other (*Please specify.*)

C5

Government A is raising capital for extension works to a power station. The country is industrialized and has a very healthy economy. A representative of the government is now meeting a representative of a foreign merchant bank, Bank B, for a preliminary discussion concerning the loan.

If you represent Government A, look on page 107 for your instructions. If you represent Bank B, look on page 108. Try to reach broad agreement on preliminary terms in accordance with the instructions you are given.

Section D   D1

Read the following telex offer sent out by Ken Bailey to several banks following the conversation with Paul Black. Then answer these questions.

1 Is the loan referred to medium-term or long-term?
2 Who is carrying out the contract in Northland?
3 What is the currency of the loan?

4 What is the interest rate on the loan?
5 Which country's laws govern the loan?

RE: STATE POWER BOARD OF NORTHLAND PLC.

KEY COMMERCIAL BANK HAS BEEN MANDATED BY THE STATE POWER BOARD OF NORTHLAND TO ARRANGE A MEDIUM-TERM LOAN FACILITY OF AROUND USD TWO HUNDRED MILLION (200,000,000) AND IS PLEASED TO INVITE YOU TO PARTICIPATE THEREIN ON THE PRINICIPAL TERMS AND CONDITIONS STATED BELOW.

BACKGROUND:

THE STATE POWER BOARD OF NORTHLAND IS A PUBLIC ELECTRIC POWER MONOPOLY WHICH SERVES THE WHOLE OF THE COUNTRY.

THE STATE POWER BOARD AND THE JOINT VENTURE STRUTZ-DILSCHMAN, COMPRISING STRUTZ AB, SWEDEN, AND DILSCHMAN PLC, UK, HAVE AS OF 10 JANUARY 1991 ENTERED INTO A CONTRACT FOR THE SUPPLY OF HIGH VOLTAGE CONVERTOR STATIONS, POWER LINE CARRIER SYSTEMS AND GROUND ELECTRODE STATIONS ON A TURNKEY BASIS FOR THE NATIONAL TRANSMISSION SYSTEM.

THE STATE POWER BOARD AND KEY COMMERCIAL BANK, LONDON, HAVE ENTERED INTO A LOAN AGREEMENT DATED 10 JANUARY 1991 FOR USD TWO HUNDRED AND FIFTY (250) MILLION, COVERING EIGHTY-FIVE (85) PER CENT OF THE CONTRACT VALUE.

THE FACILITY IN WHICH YOU ARE NOW INVITED TO PARTICIPATE FALLS WITHIN THE FRAMEWORK OF THE FIRM COMMITMENT WHICH KEY COMMERCIAL HAS MADE PURSUANT TO THE LOAN AGREEMENT OF 10 JANUARY 1991 WITH THE STATE POWER BOARD OF NORTHLAND.

BORROWER:

THE STATE POWER BOARD OF NORTHLAND

GUARANTOR:

THE FEDERAL REPUBLIC OF NORTHLAND

MANAGER AND AGENT:

KEY COMMERCIAL BANK

AMOUNT:

SUCH AMOUNT AS CAN BE SYNDICATED UP TO USD TWO HUNDRED (200) MILLION.

CURRENCY:

US DOLLARS

TERM:

EIGHT (8) YEARS

AVAILABILITY:

THE LOAN MAY BE DRAWN DOWN DURING A PERIOD COMMENCING FROM THE DATE OF THE LOAN AGREEMENT AND ENDING ON 20 MARCH 1991.

REPAYMENT:

THE AMOUNT OUTSTANDING AT THE END OF THE DRAWNDOWN PERIOD WILL BE REPAID IN TWELVE (12) ROUGHLY EQUAL SEMI-ANNUAL INSTALMENTS COMMENCING THIRTY (30) MONTHS FROM THE DATE OF DISBURSEMENT.

INTEREST RATE:

TWO AND ONE SIXTEENTH OF ONE PER CENT PER ANNUM ($2^1/_{16}$ PCT P.A.) OVER THE AVERAGE SIX-MONTH LIBOR FOR EURODOLLAR DEPOSITS. INTEREST SHALL BE PAYABLE SEMI-ANNUALLY IN ARREARS AND CALCULATED ON THE BASIS OF A THREE HUNDRED AND SIXTY (360) DAY YEAR, AND THE ACTUAL NUMBER OF DAYS ELAPSED.

MANAGEMENT FEE:

ONE AND ONE QUARTER OF ONE PER CENT ($1^1/_4$ PCT) OF THE AGGREGATE AMOUNT OF THE LOAN COMMITMENT, PAYABLE IN USD.

THE SUBSCRIPTIONS WILL BE MADE IN MULTIPLES OF USD TWO HUNDRED THOUSAND (200,000). THE MINIMUM SUBSCRIPTION IS USD TWO HUNDRED THOUSAND (200,000).

THE MANAGER RESERVES THE RIGHT TO ALLOCATE EACH LENDER'S FINAL PARTICIPATION AT ITS SOLE DISCRETION.

TAXES:

ALL PAYMENTS IN CONNECTION WITH THIS LOAN WILL BE MADE FREE AND CLEAR OF ALL PRESENT OR FUTURE NORTHLAND TAXES TO THE EXTENT SET FORTH IN THE LOAN AGREEMENT.

DOCUMENTATION AND GOVERNING LAW:

THE LOAN AGREEMENT AND THE GUARANTEE WILL BE GOVERNED BY AND CONSTRUED IN ACCORDANCE WITH THE LAWS OF ENGLAND AND CONTAIN THE NORMAL PROVISIONS FOUND IN CURRENT EUROCREDIT AGREEMENTS.

PUBLICITY:

A TOMBSTONE WILL BE PUBLISHED IF SO DESIRED BY THE PARTICIPATING BANKS.

A DRAFT OF THE LOAN AGREEMENT AND AN INFORMATION MEMORANDUM WILL BE SENT TO BANKS ON REQUEST.

PLEASE SEND CONFIRMATION OF YOUR COMMITMENT AT YOUR EARLIEST CONVENIENCE, BUT NOT LATER THAN NOON 19 FEBRUARY 1991 FOR THE ATTENTION OF MYSELF.

WITH KIND REGARDS

KEN BAILEY

FOR KEY COMMERCIAL BANK PLC, LONDON.

D2

Look at the following stages mentioned in the telex and say when they happened.

...... The beginning of the period in which the State Power Board may take up the loan facility.

...... The State Power Board signed the contract with Strutz/Dilschman.

...... Banks which want to take part in the syndicated loan must confirm their commitment to Key Commercial.

...... End of the period in which the State Power Board may take up the loan facility.

...... The State Power Board signed the loan agreement with Key Commercial.

D3

Look through the following statements and on the basis of the information in the telex say whether they are true or false.

1 It is not made clear that Key Commercial has been authorized to act on behalf of the State Power Board in raising this loan.
2 Key Commercial is itself providing at least USD 50 million of the total loan.
3 The full contract value is approximately USD 294 million.
4 The loan is without security.
5 The loan will be repaid in full by 20 September 1999 at the latest.
6 The interest rate on the loan may be different at different times.
7 Interest will be paid every six months, for the six months just gone.
8 A bank participating in the syndicated loan may provide USD 500,000.
9 Key Commercial finally decides how much each bank may provide.
10 A bank may look at the loan agreement before deciding whether to participate in the loan.

D4

You work for a bank which has received the offer telex from Key Commercial. Meet with a colleague and discuss the attraction of the telex offer. Decide on a course of action and then write a telex in reply.

D5

Most of the words in this crossword puzzle are used in Units 7 and 8.

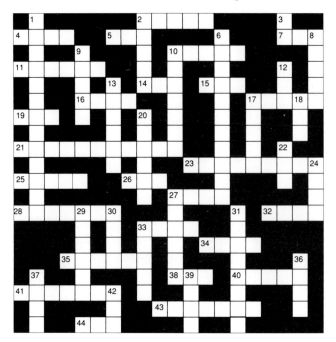

Across

2 A very big company indeed. (5)
4 Period of increasing economic activity. (4)
5 'Neither rose ... fell.' (3)
7 Dutch Guilder. (3)
10 Industrial equipment and tools. (5)
11 The beginning. (6)
14 Public limited company. (3)
15 Month. (3)
16 German currency unit. (4)
17 Commodities such as sugar, coffee and cocao. (5)
19 Gross National Product. (3)
21 Take part in. (11)
23 Offering to supply goods or services at a stated price. (9)
25 Income received from an investment. (5)
26 Deutschmark (3)
27 Amounts. (4)
28 Relating to results, e.g. for only part of a financial year. (7)
32 Prices did not rise. In fact they went ... . (4)
33 Opposite of rise. (4)
34 Document promising to pay a sum of money at a specified time. (4)
35 An area of business activity. (6)
38 Years. (3)
40 Extents of movement, e.g. 'within a £2 price ... .' (5)
41 Period of three months. (7)
43 A disappointment and difficulty. (7)
44 '... a 1990 high of $44.25 to an all-time ... of $10.' (3)

Down

1 Papers relating to a business deal. (13)
2 Several companies joined together, owned by one company. (5)
3 Billion. (2)
6 A series of regular part payments. (11)
8 Products, not services. (5)
9 Conditions of contract. (5)
10 Agreement combining several matters. (7)
12 French franc. (3)
13 A loan. (6)
17 A financial interest in a company. (5)
18 A metal. (3)
20 The parts into which the ownership of a company is divided. (6)
22 An offer to buy, at a stated price. (3)
24 An increase. (4)
27 Only, entirely. (6)
29 Turn down, say no to. (6)
30 Majority. (4)
31 Legal agreement. (8)
33 Foreign exchange. (5)
36 To act, to do business. (4)
37 Very active. (4)
39 Price level paid for the use of somebody else's money. (4)
42 Angry argument. (3)

Unit 9 Trends

International banking is a dynamic business and the changes are fast and many. What are some of the main trends? What does the future hold? In this unit we hear different bankers talking about important trends in some areas of banking and financing.

Section A   **A1**

With regard to banking in your country:

1 What are the two biggest problems?
2 What have been the two most important developments in recent years?
3 What important changes will take place in the next few years?

A2 🖭

Working with a partner, make a brief list of debt-related problems experienced by debtor countries. Then listen to Robert Aguda, who is the governor of a central bank in Africa, outlining some of the problems facing developing countries. Tick those items on your list which Robert mentions.

A3 🖭

Look through the following summaries of Robert's talk and say how you think each one finishes. Then listen to him again and check your answers.

1 The enormous economic problems facing developing countries mean that ...
2 If something is not done about the debt problems of some developing countries ...
3 Robert's country does not like taking loans because ...
4 If the external debts of the big Latin American countries were written off ...
5 In Africa, external debts are much larger ...
6 If the debts of African countries were written off ...
7 What the poorer countries of Africa need is ...
8 There should also be a worldwide dialogue in order to ...
9 A plus for some developing countries is ...
10 High interest rates mean that ...
11 These problems need special attention to ...

A4 ▦

Here are seven short sentences from Robert's talk. Each is followed by two statements that might be understood from his words. Listen to how Robert actually says these words and decide which meaning is intended.

1 Indeed recent forecasts by the IMF, the OECD and the World Bank are all far from encouraging ...
   a) ... although previous forecasts were more optimistic.
   b) ... and give very little hope for the future.
2 We ourselves are very reluctant to borrow from the markets ...
   a) ... although other countries are less reluctant.
   b) ... and try never to do it.
3 We have only to look at the debt service costs ...
   a) ... to imagine the problems which they involve.
   b) ... not to mention the total costs of repayment.
4 I believe that over 100 per cent of export earnings are required ...
   a) ... although I am not sure about this.
   b) ... and this is a very large figure indeed.
5 I think that there should be a global dialogue in order to combat inflation ...
   a) ... instead of just a few countries talking about it.
   b) ... instead of adding to it.
6 And this is, if you like, a plus for some developing countries ...
   a) ... instead of a disadvantage.
   b) ... but not for the industrialized countries.
7 These problems need very special attention ...
   a) ... but there are other problems that we can leave till later.
   b) ... no other kind of attention will help matters.

● Which words would you stress in the sentences above to give them the alternative meanings? Decide with a partner. Then read each of the sentences in one of the two ways for your partner to say whether you mean a) or b) in each case.

A5

Look at the following suggestions to overcome the problem of developing country debt. Number them in what you think is their order of importance and then compare your answer with that of a partner.

● Increase concessional aid to poorer countries.
● Begin global dialogue of economic co-operation.
● Combat inflation.
● Reduce interest rates worldwide.
● Reduce the balance of payments deficits of rich countries.
● Other. (*Please specify.*)

Section B   **B1** 🖭

Here are five general steps which Ed Walker, whom we met in Units 1 and 2, says his bank has taken to meet the debt crisis. As you listen to his presentation, number the steps in the order that Ed actually mentions them.

...... Conversion of short-term debt into long-term debt.
...... Placing of some of the largest international loans on non-accrual status.
...... Increase of reserve for credit losses to $650 million.
...... Restructuring amortizations and maturities of medium- and long-term debt.
...... Search for solutions on an individual country basis and for ways of structuring the debt.

B2 🖭

What did Ed say? Look at the list of statements below. Some are summaries of statements actually made by Ed in this section and others are not. Listen to the presentation again and put a tick (✔) against those statements that are summaries of what Ed did say.

1 The debt-servicing problems of the developing countries are going to be with us for some time to come.
2 Cybulski Bank is more affected than most other major banks by the debt crisis.
3 Banks are having to increase their capital-to-loans ratios.
4 The debt crisis is not confined to one country or even to one region.
5 Two thirds of the bank's credit losses last year were on international business loans.
6 Cybulski wants to help debtor countries to service their debt and to take further loans from the open market.
7 Public sector debt forms two thirds of Cybulski's outstandings of $950 million to Westina.
8 Interest rates on Westina's public sector debts to Cybulski are now based on LIBOR rates instead of Prime rates.
9 There are three countries with liquidity problems where the bank has outstandings which are larger than one per cent of its assets.
10 Approximately half of the bank's outstanding loans have maturities within one year.
11 It is important that an effective solution to the debt crisis is found soon.

B3

Write down the words that Ed actually uses in place of the words in *italics*.
Listen again to his presentation if you need to.

1 ... is that of the *difficulties in repaying money which is owed, together with the interest charges* ...
2 ... our own *position of risk* is less than ...
3 ... to increase our reserve for *money lost on bad debts* ...
4 ... in 1990 we *set aside for this purpose* something like 600 ...
5 ... a lot of money being used to increase *the proportion of financial resources to the amount of money lent* ...
6 ... to look for *answers* on an individual country basis.
7 ... the economic performance of *countries which owe money* ...
8 ... including the use of *low interest rates given for a special reason* ...
9 ... we've placed them *in a position where they no longer increase because of the addition of interest.*
10 The *repayments and dates when repayments become due* ...
11 ... we have *loans which have not yet been repaid* of 900 ...
12 ... some ¤÷#rds of which is *money owing from government authorities and state-owned organizations* ...
13 ... and the remainder of which is to *industrial and commercial firms which obtain loans and which are not state-owned.*
14 We've recently completed *business discussions to work out a deal* ...
15 ... have been adjusted down from *the base rate on corporate loans at big US commercial banks* plus two per cent ...
16 ... to *the average interbank offered rate for deposits in the London market* ...
17 ... one of three countries with *difficulties in meeting financial commitments* ...
18 ... outstandings *which are greater than* one per cent of our *complete worth.*
19 What the effects of this situation are going to be for the *banks which have given loans* ...

B4

Look again at the suggestions listed in A6 and B1. List what you think are the five most important points for solving international debt problems in their order of importance. Then compare your answer with that of a partner. Try to work out a new list on which you both agree.

Section C   **C1**

1 Look at the newspaper report and choose the best headline for it from this list.

Northland deregulates financial markets

High interest cheque account offered

Stockbrokers expand

Moves announced

> Stockbrokers Nelson and Hurst have received a Central Bank licence to take .... (1) , and are thus adding .... (2) banking services to their broker .... (3). The company plans a high interest call account for .... (4) customers, on which rates will be .... (5) to overnight interest rates in the money markets. A high interest cheque account is to be .... (6) for personal customers. The .... (7) is one of several announced by different companies this week, as financial institutions .... (8) for the deregulation of Northland's financial markets next year.

2 Fill the spaces with appropriate words from the box.

prepare	deposits	loans
linked	limited	offered
operations	move	corporate

C2 🖭

Colin Anderson, the chairman of a British clearing bank, talks about the changes in the banking system at a seminar.

1 Is Colin talking about changes that have already started or ones that he believes will begin in the future?
2 Do you think that Colin is positive or negative about the changes he is talking about?

C3 🖭

On the next page are the notes that someone present at the seminar took. Unfortunately not all of them are accurate. Listen again to Colin and find out what the errors are.

Seminar   Changes in institutional boundaries in the
          financial services industry

Likely to bring about a lot of changes. Probably more
important than abandonment of exchange control in
1979.

Changes so far limited to USA and UK, where there are
2 main trends:

1 formation of big financial conglomerates

2 securities houses offering something close to
   nationwide banking facilities.

Changes in UK likely. UK invisible earnings generally
good, especially banking and insurance. UK facing
competition from newly-industrialized countries. UK oil
and gas limited, but UK neglects financial services as
an important source of income. Must develop them to
replace some manufacturing industries in decline.

C4

Match the words and phrases in the left-hand column with the definitions in
the right-hand column.

1	topic	A	Meeting to exchange information and to discuss.
2	seminar	B	Main points of interest.
3	trend	C	Borders or limits which have existed for a long period of time
4	barriers	D	Income from the export of services.
5	statutory means	E	Ways connected with laws.
6	abandonment	F	Not to give attention to.
7	substantial	G	Financial organization which provides long-term loans against the security of the borrower's property.
8	peculiar to	H	Very large.
9	financial conglomerate	I	Amount of income which is higher than the amount of money spent.
10	retailing group	J	Activities in the buying and selling of land and buildings.

11 securities and commodities trading house	K Group of companies which sells goods to the public.
12 legislation	L General development or movement.
13 operations in real estate	M Growing weaker.
14 invisible earnings	N Things which maintain separation.
15 surplus	O Laws.
16 to neglect	P Giving up of something.
17 primary concerns	Q Subject, thing to be discussed.
18 in decline	R Found only in.
19 traditional demarcations	S Group of financial companies of very different kinds.
20 building society	T Company dealing in investments and raw materials such as sugar and cotton.

C5

Each of the phrases in *italics* fulfils a particular purpose. Match the phrases to the purpose.

1 *As my theme for* this seminar, I have chosen …	A Stating a point of view.
2 … *by which I mean* the trend towards …	B Explaining a word or an idea.
3 *I believe* that the consequences of this trend …	C Listing or enumerating.
4 It is, *as we will see later*, already under way …	D Leading to a logical conclusion.
5 *First*, we have seen …	E Indicating that a point will be developed later.
6 *At the same time*, securities houses have …	F Changing focus or direction.
7 *One of our primary concerns* must be to …	G Emphasizing an important topic or interest.
8 *It is for these reasons that* changes in …	H Stating something already widely known.
9 *I would like now to turn to* events …	I Indicating one event happening with another.
10 *You will of course already know* …	J Introducing the topic.

C6

Now plan a short introduction to a seminar on changes taking place in banking in your country. Try to use as many of the phrases from C4 as possible in any order you wish. A partner will listen to your introduction and will tick off the phrases that you do use.

Section D   **D1**

What do you use a computer for in your job?

*"Dammit, Miss Belknapp, you're right! –
There is a goldfish in there!!"*

D2

As preparation for the listening activities which follow, choose the best definition for the words in *italics*.

1 *Debits* are:
   a) sums of money owed by one person to another; b) records of money paid into a bank account; c) records of money taken out of a bank account.
2 *Credits* are:
   a) plastic cards used instead of money; b) sums of money paid into a bank account; c) the amount of money in a bank account.
3 The *bank's books* are:
   a) useful lists of customers' addresses and phone numbers; b) plans showing how much money the bank expects to earn and spend; c) a set of records in which the bank's accounts are kept.
4 If information is available *real time*, it is available:
   a) on a terminal very soon after being entered into the system; b) at the same time on a number of terminals linked to a central system; c) at any time of the day or night.

5 A *visual display unit* (VDU) is:
   a) a small screen that is linked to a telephone and the telephone network;
   b) a screen which shows information from a computer; c) a machine
   which shows transparencies.
6 If data is *stored on line*, it is:
   a) ready for immediate use on a central computer; b) kept on equipment
   that is not linked to a central computer; c) kept for a short time only.
7 A *database* is:
   a) the place where a company keeps its main computer; b) a room with a
   lot of computers in it; c) a large collection of data stored in a structured
   form.
8 *Advices* are:
   a) statements about what should be done; b) public notices about goods
   or services for sale; c) formal notices giving the receiver information
   about a business transaction.
9 An *interface* is:
   a) the connecting link between two computer systems; b) a place where
   someone sits to work with a computer; c) a system where two or more
   texts can appear on the screen at the same time.
10 *Enhancements* are:
   a) changes; b) improvements; c) decreases in size.
11 To *quote* prices is:
   a) to state what the prices are; b) to decide what the prices are; c) to say
   what you think the prices will be.
12 The *bank's exposure* is:
   a) how much financial risk the bank is open to; b) how much advertising
   the bank does; c) how much the bank earns.
13 If A is *on a par with* B:
   a) A is not as good as B; b) A is better than B; c) A is equal to B.
14 *back-up systems* are:
   a) groups of people who maintain and operate a computer system;
   b) systems which control the running of computers; c) systems for
   copying computer files in case the originals are damaged.
15 *Contingency planning* is about:
   a) what to do if things go wrong unexpectedly; b) how much money to
   earn and spend; c) how much money to put into bank reserves.
16 A *network* (here) is:
   a) a program which instructs a computer what to do; b) a number of
   computers in different places; c) a number of computers that are linked
   for shared use.
17 *Fraud* is:
   a) the crime of stealing money by breaking into a safe; b) the crime of
   gaining money by dishonesty; c) the crime of stealing computers.
18 *IC cards* are:
   a) identification cards; b) intelligent chip cards with built-in memories;
   c) cards with holes in them which represent data.

19 *ATM withdrawals* are:
  a) sums of money transferred to an account electronically; b) sums of money taken out of a bank account via an automatic telling machine; c) statements issued by an automatic telling machine.

D3 📼

You are going to hear Kate Morley, the manager of the currency banking unit of a British merchant bank, being interviewed about the importance of high technology in certain areas of banking. As you listen, choose the best alternative for these four sentences.

1 Kate talks / does not talk about the history of computerization in her bank.
2 Kate describes / does not describe the bank's computer systems.
3 Kate talks / does not talk about electronic funds transfer.
4 The interviewer asks / does not ask technical questions about the bank's computers.

D4

Here is a list of short courses and conferences which Kate has the opportunity to go on during the year. Based on what she says, tick the boxes for those courses you think might be of most professional interest to her.

☐ Systems for retailers
☐ Documentation for dealers
☐ Buying and paying from home
☐ Electronic trade payment
☐ Security in electronic funds transfer
☐ ATM on-line systems
☐ Risk management of foreign exchange transactions
☐ Point of sale services around the world
☐ Message transmission: strategic choices
☐ Developments in plastic cards
☐ Measuring information systems performance

D5

Read the text about electronic banking and then:

1 say whether it is mostly about equipment or about systems.
2 say how many branches are connected to the bank's network.
3 choose what you consider to be the biggest benefit provided by the bank's products.

Quintorp, one of Northland's leading banks, is to begin exporting its computerized banking systems to the USA, Europe and the Far East. The bank, which is well-known for being at the forefront of electronic banking, is confident that there is a worldwide market for its state-of-the-art solutions to the rapidly changing needs of international banking. 'What we intend to do,' says Managing Director John Seddon, 'is to make available the bank of tomorrow, that is a one-location bank which can meet all banking needs, business and retail, on the spot, by means of banking know-how combined with advanced computer technology.'

Quintorp's rise to electronic market leadership began in 1985, when it established a subsidiary company, Quintorp Computer Services, for the sole purpose of selecting hardware, developing sophisticated software applications and building a comprehensive on-line network for the bank. All of the bank's 260 domestic branches have been connected to the network since 1989, shortly after which the key branches abroad in London, Hong Kong and Bermuda went on-line. The bank's other international branches in 21 countries were linked to the network in 1990. More than 2,000 AJS/500 terminals have been installed in the network, with control and data being concentrated at the host site.

Among the real-time software packages which the bank has designed and operated, and which it now intends to market, is the Sylvia system. This integrates a dealing function, global interbank telex and telecommunications systems, a branch system including management, clerical and teller functions and an ATM function. A notable application module in the Sylvia system is the dealing room package, which aids dealer performance by providing currency positions and other real-time data such as cash flow management and automatic confirmation of deals.

A portfolio and trust management system is also available, which includes a securities facility providing an on-line real-time connection to the Northland stock exchange. Purchases can be made via a terminal, and the whole operation is paperless.

A feature which Quintorp is developing as part of its concept of tomorrow's bank is a display service whereby corporate customers will be able to interface personal computers directly with the bank's network by means of the telephone line and a modem. The up-to-the-minute information thus available will include direct linking facilities via the modem to domestic and foreign stock exchanges.

The bank's priority investments in electronic banking have produced what Seddon describes as 'advanced equipment and systems, which have facilitated increased administrative control, rationalization of clerical duties, and expanded information gathering capabilities, all of which means quicker, more reliable, and increased customer services'. Potential purchasers of the bank's electronic products could do worse than look at the impressive growth in Quintorp's earnings during recent years.

D6

John Seddon speaks about meeting 'all banking needs, business and retail'. Now make two separate lists of products and services offered by the bank to meet these needs, one list about banking for business customers and the other list about retail banking.

D7

1 What are the general trends in banking and finance in your country?
2 What are the trends in your bank or organization in particular?

Role play instructions

Unit 3 C8

Dealer, Bank B

The US dollar has been steady for a couple of days. The dollar/Deutschmark interbank rate is 1.9055 (buy) and 1.9060 (sell). You believe, however, that the dollar will rise during the day, probably by a pfennig or so.

Unit 4 C5

Bank B

You have some news for your customer: your bank's base rate is being increased by ½% next week to 10½%. Your margins in general are about right – you could afford to decrease them a little, but not by too much.

Unit 6 C4

Bank Z

Delays in payment are not your fault – your Central Bank makes it tough for you, because of the country's lack of foreign exchange. Your position is:

- You think it would be fair to pay Bank A interest costs on delays in the payment of confirmed documentary credits, at the LIBOR rate, for half of the average delay period, i.e. 20 days.
- You would also like to increase the line that Bank A has established for you for the confirmation of credits, from USD 2 million to USD 3 million.
- You want to increase your business in general with Bank A, as your national economy is beginning to pick up, due to the fact that machinery is now being exported more and more.

Unit 8 C5

Government A

Bank B is the second bank that you have met this week to discuss this loan, as you met Bank X yesterday. You need $55 million, and Bank X has indicated that it can lend you this sum, as the sole provider. They suggest two tranches: firstly a ten year loan, at a fixed rate of interest of 10½% per annum, with semi-annual repayments, and secondly a bullet repayment of $15 million after two years. Now see if you can get better terms from Bank B.

Unit 3 C8

Cash Manager, Company C

You are almost sure that your company will need to buy USD 1 million later today, spot, with Deutschmarks. The dollar has been steady all this week, and at present you know the dollar/Deutschmark rate to be around 1.9055.

Unit 4 C5

Company C

Your company is becoming very cost conscious. You have been through Bank B's charges with your boss, and he wants you to reduce them overall by at least 10%. See what you can do.

Unit 6 C4

Bank A

● With regard to delays in the payment of confirmed documentary credits by Bank Z, you want interest paid for the first 30 days at the LIBOR rate. For above 30 days, you suggest LIBOR plus 1%.
● You want the outstanding £95,000 paid immediately – never mind any interest.
● You want to decrease the line that you have established for Bank Z for the confirmation of credits, from USD 2 million to USD 1 million, unless Bank Z is fairly helpful on the above points.

Unit 8 C5

Bank B

You can lend up to £30 million as the sole provider. Your suggestion is an eight year loan, at a fixed rate of interest of 11½% per annum, with quarterly repayments. If the sum is more than £30 million, you will have to syndicate the loan. In this case, you will have to increase the interest rate. Find out how you can best help Government A.

List of abbreviations

Here is a list of abbreviations you are likely to meet in the world of banking and finance, some of which are included in the units of this book. Please note that the list is not comprehensive and that you may meet the abbreviations in a slightly different form, for example *A/d* meaning *After date* could be written *a.d.*.

A
A/C   Account
Acc.   Account *or* Accept
ACH   Automated clearing house
Ack.   Acknowledge, acknowledgement
Ackgt.   Acknowledgement
Acpt.   Accept, acceptance
Acrd.   Accrued
Ac. Pay. Accounts payable
Ac. Rec. Accounts receivable
ACT   Advance corporation tax
A/d   After date
Add.   Addition, addendum
Adv.   Advance *or* Advice
Advsd.   Advised
Affil.   Affiliate
AFT   Automatic fund transfer
Aft.   After
Agd.   Agreed
AGI   Adjusted gross income
Agt.   Agent *or* Agreement
AI   Accrued interest *or* Accumulated interest
AL   Accrued liabilities
A/m   Above-mentioned
Amt.   Amount
Ann.   Annual *or* Annuity
A/or   And/or
Approx.   Approximately
APR   Annual percentage rate
Appr.   Approximately
AR   Accounts receivable *or* Annual report *or* Annual return

Assmt.   Assessment
ATM   Automatic telling machine, automated teller machine
Att.   Attached
Aud.   Audit, Auditor
AUD   Australian dollar
Auth.   Authority
Av.   Average
Avg.   Average
AY   Annual yield

B
Bal.   Balance
Bd.   Board *or* Bond
B/D   Bank draft
B/d   Brought down
B/Dft.   Bank draft
B/E   Bill of exchange
BEF   Belgian franc
B/f   Brought forward
Bfcy.   Beneficiary
Bgt.   Bought
Bk.   Bank
Bkg.   Banking
Bkr.   Broker
Bkrpt.   Bankrupt
Bks.   Books
B/L   Bill of lading
Bn   Billion
BP   Bills payable *or* Book profit
BR   Bills receivable *or* Bond rating *or* Bank rate
Br.   Branch
Brok.   Broker, brokerage
BS   Balance sheet *or* Bill of sale
BV   Book value
BW   Bid wanted

C
CA   Capital assets *or* Current assets
CAD   Canadian dollar *or* Cash against documents
Canc.   Cancellation

Cap.   Capital, capitalization
CC   Cancellation clause
CCA   Current cost accounting
CCE   Current cash equivalent
CCY   Convertible currency
CD   Certificate of deposit
C/d   Carried down
Cert.   Certificate
C/f   Carried forward
C&F   Cost and freight
CF   Cash flow
CFA   Cash flow accounting
Cfm.   Confirm
CFR   Cost and freight
CGT   Capital gains tax
CHAPS   Clearing house automated payment system
CHF   Swiss franc
Chge.   Charge
CHIPS   Clearing house interbank payment system
Chq.   Cheque
CI   Cash items *or* Compound interest
CIF   Cost, insurance, freight
CIP   Freight or carriage and insurance paid
CL   Call loan *or* Capital loss *or* Current liabilities
Cl   Clause
CLOC   Clean letter of credit
Cmdty.   Commodity
Cmm.   Commission
Cn.   Consolidated
Cncld.   Cancelled
Co.   Company
COD   Cash on delivery
Col.   Column
Coll.   Collection *or* Collateral
Collat.   Collateral
Com'l ppr.   Commercial paper
COMECON   Council of Mutual Economic Assistance
Comm.   Commission
Conds.   Conditions

Consgt. Consignment
COP Current operating profit
Corp. Corporation
CP Closing price *or* Commercial paper
CPI Consumer price index
Cr. Credit, creditor
CT Cash transfer
Cum. Cumulative
Cur. Currency
Cy. Currency
CY Current yield

D
D/A Documents against acceptance
DAF Delivered at frontier
Db. Debenture
DCP Freight or carriage to (named port)
DD Due date
DDA Demand deposit account
DDP Delivered duty paid
Deb. Debenture
Def. Deficit
Dem. Demand
DEM Deutschmark
Dep. Deposit
Dept. Department
DES Data encryption standard
Dis. Discount
Disb. Disbursement
Div. Division *or* Dividend
DKK Danish krone
Dir. Dealer
Dly. Daily
DM Deutschmark
DNI Distributable net income
DOG Days of grace
Dol. Dollar
DP Data processing *or* Documents against payment
DR Discount rate
D/S Days after sight
DTBA Date to be advised

E
EBIT Earnings before interest and taxes
EC European Community
ECGD Export Credit Guarantees department
ECU European currency unit

EE Equity earnings
E&e Each and every
EEC European Economic Community
EFT Electronic funds transfer
EFTA European Free Trade Association
EFTPOS Electronic funds transfer point of sale
EFTS Electronic funds transfer system
EI Earned income
EMS European Monetary System
E&OE Errors and omissions accepted
EOM End of month
EPOS Electronic point of sale
EPS Earnings per share
Equ. Equity
ES Earned surplus
ESP Spanish peseta
Ex. Exchange
Exch. Exchange
Excl. Excluding
Exp. Expense *or* Export
EXQ Ex quay
EXS Ex ship
EXW Ex works

F
FA Fixed assets *or* Floating assets *or* Face amount
FAS Free alongside ship
FB Fidelity bond
FC Fixed capital *or* Fixed charges *or* Futures contract
FCV Full contract value
FE Foreign exchange
FI Foreign investment
Fin. Finance
FOA FOB airport
FOB Free on board *or* Freight on board
FOR Free on rail
Forex Foreign exchange
FP Fixed price
FRC Free carrier (named port)
FRCD Floating-rate certificate of deposit
FRF French franc
FRN Floating-rate note
FS Financial statement

FV Face value
F/X Foreign exchange
FY Fiscal year
FYG For your guidance
FYI For your information

G
GA General average *or* Gross asset
GATT General Agreement on Tariffs and Trade
GBP British pound
GDP Gross domestic product
GE Gross earnings
Gen. Led. General ledger
GNP Gross national product
GP Gross profit *or* Grace period
Gp. Group
GR Gross receipts, gross revenue
GS Government securities *or* Gross sales
GTC Good till cancelled
Gtd. Guaranteed
Guar. Guarantee

H
HC Holding company

I
IBELS Interest-bearing eligible liabilities
IC Intelligent chip
IDB Inter-dealer broker
I.f. In full
II Institutional investor
IMF International Monetary Fund
Imp. Import
In. Income
Inc. Income *or* Incorporated
Incl. Including
Inst. Instant *or* Instalment
Inv. Invoice
IS Income statement
IT Income tax
ITL Italian lire

J
JPY Japanese yen
JV Joint venture

L
LA Liquid assets

LAFTA   Latin American Free Trade Association
LC   Loan capital
L/C   Letter of credit *or* Line of credit
LDC   Less developed country
LDT   Licensed deposit-taker
Led.   Ledger
Li.   Liabilities
LIBOR   London Interbank Offered Rate
LIFFE   London International Financial Futures Exchange
LL   Limited liability
LME   London Metal Exchange
LOC   Letter of Credit
LR   Loan rate
LS   Listed securities (stocks)
Ltd.   Limited

M
M   Million
MAC   Message authentication code
Marg.   Margin
Mat.   Maturity, matured
MB   Municipal bond *or* Merchant bank
MD   Maturity date
Misc.   Miscellaneous
Mkt.   Market
MLR   Minimum lending rate
MMC   Money market certificate
Mtg.   Meeting
Mthly.   Monthly
Mths.   Months

N
N/A   Not applicable *or* Not available *or* Non-acceptance
NA   Net assets *or* Nostro account
NAV   Net asset value
NC   Net capital *or* Net cost
NCF   Net cash flow
ND   Net debt
NE   Net earnings
N.e.   Not exceeding
Negb.   Negotiable
NH   New high
NI   Net income *or* Negotiable instrument *or* Net interest
NL   Net loss

NLG   Dutch guilder
No.   Number
NOK   Norwegian Krone
NP   Net position *or* Net profit
NPV   Net present value
NRV   Net realizable value
NS   Net surplus
N.S.   Not specified *or* Not sufficient (funds)
NW   Net worth
NWC   Net working capital
NY   Net yield

O
OB   Operating budget
O/b   On or before
OBU   Offshore banking unit
OC   Operating company *or* Organizational chart
OD   On demand *or* Overdraft *or* Overdraw *or* Overdue
OE   Operating expense
OECD   Organization for Economic Cooperation and Development
OF   Offshore funds
Ofd.   Offered
OI   Operating income *or* Ordinary interest
OL   Operating losses
OP   Operating profit *or* Offering price *or* Opening price
OPEC   Organization of Petroleum Exporting Countries
Opt.   Option
OR   Operating reserves
O/S   Outstanding
OTC   Over the counter
Outstg.   Outstanding

P
PA   Paying agent *or* Power of attorney *or* Per annum
PAC   Put and call (option)
PAN   Primary account number
PAP   Pre-arranged payment
Part.   Participation
Payt.   Payment
Pce.   Piece
Pcs.   Pieces *or* prices
Pct.   Per cent
Pd.   Paid
PD   For each day

PE   Price-earnings ratio
PER   Par exchange rate *or* Price-earnings ratio
Per. Cap.   Per capita
Pfd.   Preferred
PI   Prime interest (rate)
PIN   Personal identification number
P & L   Profit and loss
PLC   Public Limited Company
PN   Promissory note
POS   Point of sale
PP   Purchase price *or* Partial payment *or* Paper profit *or* Pages *or* On behalf of (per procuration) *or* Prompt payment
Pr.   Preferred *or* Principal
PR   Pro rata
Prin   Principal
PSBR   Public sector borrowing requirement
PSL   Private sector liquidity
PTE   Pretax earnings
PV   Par value *or* Present value
PY   Prior year
Pymt.   Payment

Q
QA   Quick assets
QP   Quoted price
Qtly.   Quarterly
Qtr.   Quarter
Qy.   Query

R
RC   Recurring charges *or* Reserve currency *or* Risk currency *or* Replacement costs
Rcd.   Received
Rcpt.   Receipt
RE   Rate of exchange *or* Real estate
Re.   Regarding
Recd.   Received
Redem.   Redemption
Ref.   Reference *or* Refunding
Regd.   Registered
Regs.   Regulations
Rem.   Remittance
REPO   Repurchasing agreement
Res.   Reserve
Rev. a/c   Revenue account
RFP   Request for proposal

RFQ   Request for quotation
Rmdr.   Remainder
ROA   Return on assets
ROCE   Return on capital employed
ROE   Rate of exchange *or* Return on equity
ROI   Return on investment
ROR   Rate of return
RPI   Retail price index
RPQ   Request for price quotation
RR   Required reserves
Rt.   Right
RTBA   Rate to be agreed

S
S/A   Subject to acceptance
SAN   Subsidiary account number
SC   Stock certificate
SD   Sight draft *or* Stock dividend
SDR   Special drawing rights
SE   Stock exchange
SEK   Swedish krona
Shr.   Share
SI   Simple interest
Sig.   Signature
Sk   safekeeping
S & L   Assn. Savings and loan association
Sld.   Sold
SM   Secondary market
SO   Seller's option *or* Standing order *or* Stock option
SOE   Short of exchange
SP   Selling price *or* Spot price *or* Stop payment
Ster.   Sterling
Suby.   Subsidiary
Sur.   Surplus

T
TA   Tangible assets
TBA   To be advised *or* To be agreed
T bill   Treasury bili
T bond   Treasury bond
TI   Taxable income
TL   Time loan
TN   Transferable notice
T note   Treasury note
TO   Treasury obligation
T/O   Turnover

Tot.   Total
TR   Tax rate *or* Trust receipt
Tr.   Trust
Treas.   Treasurer, treasury
Trf.   Transfer
TS   Tax shelter *or* Treasury stock
T/T   Telegraphic transfer

U
UNI   Undistributed net income
Unpd.   Unpaid
UOT   Unit of trading
UP   Unrealized profits
USD   US dollar
USM   Unlisted securities market

V
Val.   Value
VAT   Value-added tax
VC   Venture capital
VCF   Venture capital funds
VD   Volume discount
VDU   Visual display unit

W
WDV   Written down value
WEF   With effect from
WR   Warehouse receipt
W/W   Worldwide

X
X ch.   Exchange
X cl.   Excess current liabilities
X in.   Excluding interest

Y
Yr.   Year *or* Your

Acknowledgements

The author and publishers are grateful to the following copyright owners for permission to reproduce photographs and cartoons.

page 1: Businesswoman – The Telegraph Colour Library; Businessman – ZEFA; Businessman – Tony Stone Photo Library
page 3: Dealing Room – Tony Stone Photo Library
page 34: Meeting – The Telegraph Colour Library
page 47: Presentation – Tony Stone Photo Library
page 58: Cargo Plane – The International Stock Exchange Photo Library; Container ship – ZEFA
page 70: Finance – Art Directors Photo Library
page 82: Dam – The J. Allan Cash Photolibrary; Bridge – Department of the Environment for Northern Ireland/ Graphic Design Service
page 102: Cartoon – Private Eye

Picture research by Sandie Huskinson-Rolfe, Photoseekers

Book design by Ken Brooks Design Services

Notes